T0285627

Caged

CAGED

A Teacher's Journey Through Rikers, or How I Beheaded the Minotaur

Brandon Dean Lamson

EMPIRE STATE EDITIONS

AN IMPRINT OF FORDHAM UNIVERSITY PRESS

NEW YORK   2023

Fordham University Press has no responsibility for the persistence or accuracy of URLs for external or third-party Internet websites referred to in this publication and does not guarantee that any content on such websites is, or will remain, accurate or appropriate.

Fordham University Press also publishes its books in a variety of electronic formats. Some content that appears in print may not be available in electronic books.

Visit us online at www.fordhampress.com/empire-state-editions.

Library of Congress Cataloging-in-Publication Data available online at https://catalog.loc.gov.

Printed in the United States of America

25 24 23   5 4 3 2 1

First edition

For all of the students I taught on Rikers

And for Elizabeth, always

CONTENTS

I decided to live with my head down and to follow my destiny by going towards the night, exactly the opposite of you, and to exploit the other of your beauty.

—Jean Genet

Part I

FALLING

Part 1

FALLING

The Weapons Board

I WASN'T PREPARED for the way this suffering was written on bodies. Skulls indented by pipes, faces disfigured by helixes of scar tissue, keloids twisting like pale worms. A buck fifty meant one hundred and fifty stitches; a smiley, supposedly given to snitches, ran from below the ear all the way to the outer lip, following the jaw line, gruesomely tracing another mouth. I cannot count the number of beautiful young men whose faces were mutilated this way, the scars that crossed their faces like stitches on a baseball more noticeable against their coppery skin. Three burns on the webbing between the forefinger and thumb represented membership in the Bloods. Tattooed tears stood for homicides or "bodies," as in "How many bodies you got, son?" Despite the answer, ultimately they all had only one: one three-dimensional surface to deface, burn, and tag with script. One brain to absorb blows and recognize enemies, one heart to guard or gradually open, one rhythm to listen to, whose incessant beat meant they were still alive.

New civilian employees on Rikers Island were sent to a mandatory orientation given by the Gang Task Force. We were told about the major gangs on the island: the Bloods, the Latin Kings, the Netas, and the Jamaican Posse. The Kings and the Bloods were frequently at war, with a shift in power over the past decade that placed the Bloods on top. I learned how to recognize gang hand signs and trademark tattoos and scars. Inverted *b*s formed by forefinger and thumb signaled Bloods, and lotus-shaped crowns made by both hands signaled Latin Kings. A triangle of three dots burned into the skin with cigarettes signified Bloods, tattooed tears the bodies of enemies slain. Those giving the orientation probably also told us about common gang terminology, though my attention must have drifted, because my ignorance about these terms would soon be exposed.

The main attraction of our orientation session was the weapons board: a four- by six-foot board that displayed weapons confiscated during various searches. Rusty shanks, razors, lengths of pipe, brass knuckles, screwdrivers with handles of tape, chains with padlocks, loops of metal wire. As I looked, I remembered the huge sharks-tooth board that hung on a wall in my grandparents' cabin, filled with prehistoric incisors, each of them labeled according to genus and species. Like those teeth, these makeshift weapons were archetypes, each one representing dozens of others that hadn't been found. Their origins numerous and untraceable, these weapons were smuggled in during visits or by the guards, fashioned from steel braces under desktops and chair legs stolen from classrooms or counseling offices. They were portable, carried under tongues or wrapped and inserted into rectums, an act called boofing. Often inmates practiced first with metal tabs from soda cans, holding them under their tongues and even sleeping with them in their mouths before they graduated to razors.

The guard who was propping up the weapons board conveyed this information in a low monotone that did not communicate concern for our safety. He was tall, his pale cheeks scarred by acne, inflamed under fluorescent lights as he displayed the weapons board and lectured to us scared civilians.

"Be aware of your surroundings at all times," he intoned. "Do not turn your back on these inmates. If you do, you make yourself vulnerable to attack. Do not make the mistake of believing they are your friends. They will test you. They will ask you to do things for them. Little things, small favors. Do not do them. I repeat, do not indulge inmates' requests. They do not have your interests in mind, only theirs. These weapons were all found in prisoners' cells. Most of them were made from items smuggled into the prison by civilians. If you suspect an inmate has a weapon, report it immediately to a commanding officer. Do not confront the inmate yourself. I repeat, do not confront them. Help us to do our job. Be alert. Be vigilant. Do not forget where you are."

The guard's speech did not console me. I suspected that he enjoyed frightening us before telling us what to do, but I also understood that he'd been told to deliver it because he was experienced and had proven himself on the job. Soon it would be time for me to do the same.

Killer Inside

MY FIRST RELATIONSHIP with a murderer was with Ward, my high school chemistry partner. Quiet and easy-going, with an open smile and a pock-marked face, he was easy for me to talk to, and we soon became friends.

A year older than I and one of the few Black kids accepted by the white preppie crowd, he'd surely seen me leaning on a wall between classes sporting my Adidas sweatsuit and gold chains, the one white boy who hung with the Black kids. Although in the classroom I was close with Ward, our friendship didn't extend out into the hallways where the theoretical laws of physics became real cause and effect.

Ward killed a girl in our class. Here's what happened: He'd borrowed some books from this kid Eric Green, a star football player whose sister Amanda he was also friends with. One day Ward called the Greens' house, knowing that Eric and his parents were away on a trip, and asked if he could come by to drop off some books. Amanda said sure, and when he arrived, she opened the door to glimpse a hunting rifle pointed at her face. Luckily, she was able to turn and run, and the first shot missed her. Not so fortunate was her friend Katie, who had agreed to spend the night at her house so Amanda wouldn't be alone. She was shot point-blank in the face.

After he shot Katie, Ward chased Amanda through the house and into the woods, continuing to fire rounds into the bank of trees. She escaped. He returned to his car, drove to a pharmacy, and purchased a bottle of NoDoz. He swallowed all of them, believing the overdose would kill him. When he was arrested, he claimed that voices told him the girls were demons

5

that he needed to destroy. His uncle had taught him about the voices and how to listen to them. His court-appointed attorney attempted to file an insanity plea with the court, but the plea was denied.

I didn't need to do extensive research to learn about this case. I read a copy of the actual file, including a transcript of the court psychologist's interview with Ward. My father, still a District Court judge at the time, laid the copied file in front of me after he told me what had happened. If I hadn't read it, I wouldn't have believed it, naïve as I was about mental illness. Even then I was outraged by the denial of Ward's insanity plea, sure that if I had been in his position my plea would have been accepted. My father agreed, but the ruling judge was not persuaded by Ward's talk of demons and voices, perhaps influenced by the racial charge of a case in which a Black boy killed a white girl in a small southern community where I remember seeing recruitment fliers for the Ku Klux Klan nailed to telephone poles. Racism in the county I grew up in was blatant and pervasive, advertised where even children could see it. It permeated every institution: the Methodist church my family attended, my private school that was founded the year that public schools were desegregated, and especially the court where my father presided.

Once, he drove me to the repair shop that one of his friends owned. He rolled down the window and Mattingly placed his greasy hands on the car door. "What about those niggers," he said, and my father nodded. I was twelve, old enough to know the meaning of that word, a word I'd never heard my father say. As we pulled back onto the road I was furious, ashamed by his passivity, and I asked, "Why didn't you say anything to him when he used that word?" My father told me to mind my business, that no one had been speaking to me.

I was also in his courtroom a year later when a white officer went on trial for assaulting my soccer coach. The officer was well known in the county and friendly with my father. He was the repeated winner of the Strongest Cop Competition, held every year at North Beach. When he was a child, he'd had an accident with gasoline in a neighbor's basement, and his chest and back were covered with scars. I imagined that these wounds disfiguring his torso explained his violence in some way.

According to my coach, who was Black, the officer called him a racial slur and struck him repeatedly after a routine traffic stop. I loved my coach; all of the kids on the team did. He was gentle with us when we made mistakes, always encouraging. And I knew that he was an honest man.

As he testified, his eye still blackened from the beating, I wanted to fast-forward the trial to hear the guilty verdict. My coach had not been alone: A friend of his, also Black, had been in the car, and he testified next, corroborating what my coach had said. I naïvely believed that would make a difference. It wasn't just one person's word against another's; a witness had been present. Finally the officer took the stand and denied everything. My father listened, called for a recess, and returned a few minutes later. As he pronounced "Not guilty," striking the gavel, the air was sucked from the chamber, from my lungs. The disbelief on my coach's face was heartbreaking. I felt somehow complicit, dirtied by it, as though I'd made a mistake as the officer sauntered down the aisle. Years later, he was elected County Sheriff. I never spoke to my father about it afterward; I just couldn't.

Why did my father show me Ward's file? To help me make sense of the inexplicable or to prove that he knew more than I did, his judgement unquestionable? Later, did I choose to teach in prison to help people like my friend or to prove something to myself, that I wasn't afraid to go where my father had sent innocent and guilty folks alike?

One-third of the prisoners on Rikers Island have been diagnosed with a mental illness. The majority of them are untreated, making Rikers the largest and possibly least effective in-patient psychiatric unit in New York. Especially in the fall when the weather turns cold, a number of mentally ill homeless folks commit petty crimes and get sent to the Island where they receive shelter and meals. The other inmates refer to them as trolls, and they are usually undisturbed as they roam through the cell blocks wrapped in filthy blankets, muttering to themselves. Most prisoners who struggle with mental illness are not so recognizable, and they suffer silently as Ward did. Though I wasn't aware of it when I started the job, teaching at Rikers was as much counseling as classroom instruction, especially once the inmates began to trust me and their inner worlds began to leak through their façades.

I moved to Manhattan in January, sleeping on the couch in my brother's SoHo apartment until his roommate insisted that I move out several weeks later. I checked into a welfare hotel next to the Hudson River where the cheapest rooms were fifteen bucks a night. I paid for two nights in a six- by nine-foot plywood box whose ceiling was made of chicken wire. It was a trough, really, and I've found when you sleep in a trough, God starts to speak to you. If you're a composer, perhaps you discover your great themes. If you're a physician, maybe you stumble upon an elusive cure. I pulled a yellow legal pad from my duffel bag and began writing in the anemic light of my urban chicken coop. Whatever dictation I received from the muses didn't survive but soothed me enough to bundle up and walk to the corner deli for a fifty-cent coffee as I contemplated my circumstances.

My writing life began with a train ride. My brother's high school English teacher, a graduate of the Iowa Writers' Workshop, was taking a train back to Maryland when she recognized the man sitting across the aisle. He was Stanley Plumly, a renowned poet who'd taught at Iowa and was now at the University of Maryland, where I'd enrolled as a freshman in the fall. She told my brother that I should try to take a class with Stan. Luckily for me, he was scheduled to teach that following spring the first undergraduate class that he'd taught in years, an introduction to poetry course. I got in and he took notice of the papers I wrote on Sylvia Plath's "Sheep in Fog" and Elizabeth Bishop's "At the Fishhouses." At the end of the semester he asked, "Hey kid, have you ever thought about writing poems?" I had, and I already was, although I was too shy to tell him that. He directed me to take a workshop with one of his talented graduate students, David Biespiel, and arranged for us to do a semester-long independent study course on Robert Penn Warren's poetry. Meeting with Stanley every week in his office and talking about Warren's poems was a wonderful gift. Eventually I took a workshop with him, and in class he described one of my failed poems as two guys dressed up in a horse suit pretending to be a horse. After I graduated, he guided me to the Creative Writing Program at Indiana University. Now, with my MFA in hand I was trying to figure out how to live as a writer in New York, an unfamiliar and overwhelming city, one in which I was currently homeless.

After scouring the paper for the numbers of rental agencies, I started making phone calls, leaving voicemails in the days when answering machines were ubiquitous. One night, a purple bath towel wrapped around me, I trudged down the corridor in my flip-flops toward the communal shower. Wind gusted through the cracks of the doors, a low whistling. I listened for human sounds behind the paper-thin walls, wishing for privacy but also to be comforted. Back in my own room the temperature plummeted as the winter night deepened, and I prayed for something to break in my favor.

The next day I walked into a rental agency in on Bleecker Street in Greenwich Village. The woman sitting at the desk told me there was one available studio apartment she could show me. She warned me that it was quite small. Not as small as my chicken coop, I thought. She handed me the keys and told me the address: 226 West 13th Street. I found the building and walked down three steps to the entrance. After a short walk through the hallway, I exited the back door and saw a three-story brick carriage house nestled between taller buildings. Climbing the wood stairs, I imagined I'd discovered a secret hideout or clubhouse, and in a sense I had. Formerly used as slave quarters and then as illegal drinking spots during Prohibition, these structures were remnants of a hidden city, one that was haunted and in ruin. Unlocking the door at the top of the stairs, I stepped inside.

It was tiny, even by Manhattan standards. I could barely stand beneath the room's slanted ceiling. The entire studio was maybe ten by fourteen feet. Enough space for a bed, a stereo, a table, and a chair. Thankfully, there was a separate bathroom and a mini-fridge. Windows on two sides of the studio faced the surrounding apartment buildings. Could I really live here? As I sat on the floor, images flashed by: the chicken wire ceiling, the chill of the cold cement as I walked down the hallway after a shower, ghostly voices drifting from transistor radios. Yes, I could do it for a few months. I didn't have much choice. It was only temporary, a pause before I could find something better.

I got the apartment, and it didn't take long for me to move my few possessions into the carriage house. I bought a futon, a small table inlaid with blue tiles, and a folding chair. With the exception of my old stereo, those were all of my furnishings. Books I stacked in a corner on the floor or in boxes on the landing outside my door. A few of my clothes fit in the sliver of a closet; the rest joined my library on the landing.

A few weeks after I moved into the studio, my brother called. He knew I was looking for a full-time teaching job. His new girlfriend was a teacher and thought she could hook me up. I met her that night at El Sombrero, a Mexican joint on 4th Street whose main attraction was the lethally potent margaritas they served for two dollars each every day from four to seven. The decor of El Sombrero resembled the inside of a pinball machine, flashing strands of red and green lights festooning its late-afternoon gloom.

She was sitting on a barstool, her dirty-blond hair spilling over her shoulders, and as she stood up to greet me I realized how tall she was. I liked my brother's new girlfriend immediately. Paige had grown up on Long Island, in a house with her alcoholic German parents and her younger brother, Max. She referred to her family's traumatic domestic situation as "the crime scene." After graduating from NYU, she enlisted in the Peace Corps and spent two years in Madagascar. Paige reminded me of my favorite aunt: statuesque, dirty-blond, and a talker. She said she wanted to ask me something, leaning forward, the pepper lights flashing across her cheeks.

"Want to work with me at a new school that just opened up called Horizon Academy? It's located on Rikers."

"Rikers Island?"

"Yes, that's it, the Island, the Rock," she said, smiling.

"The prison?"

"That's correct; your brother told me you were sharp. Listen, the principal is amazing, and she'll let you design your own courses and order your own materials. The school serves inmates between eighteen and twenty-one. The schedule is fantastic. I teach five days a week from eleven to four. The only pain in the ass is the commute. You have to take the subway to Queens Plaza, then the Q101 bus that goes directly to Rikers. Why don't you come with me one day, meet Gloria, and see if you're interested."

Later, I realized Paige had given me the hard sell. She hadn't needed to. If you'd asked me then why I applied for a job teaching in prison, I would have said it was because I needed the money. Or I would have said it's just temporary, like my cramped studio apartment at the top floor of a carriage house. I may have claimed it was an adventure that offered an escape from the drudgery of nine-to-five office jobs, an irresistible storyline to repeat in bars or at interviews. On the surface, all of these claims were true.

I met Paige early one morning outside the subway station at 4th Street and Sixth Avenue. Guiding me to the bagel shop nearby, she shared with me her morning ritual of a bagel and hazelnut coffee. Then we plunged down the stairs into the tunnels, steam rising from grates, through the turnstile and onto a platform. Paige did this gracefully, somehow juggling her coffee, bagel, wallet, and MetroCard while I stopped, stumbled, and tried to not spill my breakfast on the floor.

A thin man, dressed in a camouflage jacket shellacked with grime and threadbare pants, approached Paige on the platform while I lagged behind. Suddenly she yelled, and I saw that the man had taken her cup of coffee. Dropping my briefcase, I grabbed the front of his jacket and shoved him against an iron beam, feeling his slender frame give. I pulled the cup from his hand, stared at his squashed nose and gray whiskers, his lips sunken around toothless gums. His breath reeked of malt liquor, and a bloodshot film hung over his eyes. He shuffled away, muttering.

"Go away," I said softly, letting him disappear into the caverns of warm rushing air, mazes of tunnels where homeless camps hack space out of several feet of darkness surrounding the rails. Maybe he was seeking warmth after a night huddled in a cardboard refrigerator box—a box that had contained one of the new models, not the old heavy steel goliaths my parents had warned me about, dozens of rusting General Electric models abandoned in a junkyard near our house. I knew about kids who'd been accidentally locked inside them, suffocating in the insulated chamber where meats had been kept pink and fresh. Days later they were found, blue and swollen. I'd wondered if they knew they'd never get out, or if, as their oxygen dwindled, they kept beating the door with their fists and feet, praying it would spring open.

During the subway ride to Queens Plaza, Paige called me her hero and asked what I'd been thinking, how I had acted so quickly. I wasn't thinking anything, I told her; it was completely instinctual. As she continued to praise me, I used her story to fashion another plate of armor to cover myself with. Where I was going I'd need it, but in that moment I wished I'd given that man my cup of coffee.

Island Bound

QUEENS PLAZA. A stone's throw from Queensbridge, home to the rappers Nas and Mobb Deep. We waited at the stop for the Q101 bus to Rikers Island: family members and girlfriends, teachers and counselors, all of us standing in line for the Q101 to ferry us over the one bridge that connected Queens to the island.

The Styrofoam coffee cups we clutched in our frigid hands signaled we belonged elsewhere and were choosing to venture into a place of punishment and suffering forgotten by our fellow citizens. I knew nothing that first morning of what awaited me or, once I encountered it, whether I would return. Grabbing me by the wrist, Paige guided me toward the bus as it arrived, and we climbed its pneumatic steps.

Usually the Q101 was packed, especially Wednesday through Friday, the busiest visiting days. Passengers shoved their way onboard, the last ones standing in the aisle shoulder to shoulder, most of them women going to visit their men, a handful of former inmates returning to pick up their property or to see their friends, and a few fellow civilians who were social workers or drug counselors. Even a few guards rode the bus, though talk about lions and lambs: Although the guards were the bosses inside prison walls, riding the bus they became vulnerable, surrounded by the family and friends of those they lorded over behind bars. Once I was a regular on the Q101 I became accustomed to the claustrophobic energy on the bus, the crushing despair that held us in place like those amusement park centrifuge rides that spin screaming riders in the dark.

I drank the rest of my Dunkin's coffee, staring out of the scratched bus windows as we approached the bridge to the island. Around me, passengers sank deeper into their fleece coats. A woman three seats behind us leaned over and dumped the contents of a large envelope into the aisle, then lit a match and tossed it onto the pile of photos. Images of her loved one's former selves, a young man in a shark-gray suit posing with his prom date, writhed and curled into angry fists of charred paper.

Passengers yelled to the bus driver to pull over, which he did not. Another woman stood up, ripped the lid off her large coffee, and poured it on the flaming pictures that hissed and smoked. I asked Paige if things like this happened often on the Q101. "Every day, chief," she replied. One thing I appreciated about Paige was her stoic humor during a crisis and the speed at which a sarcastic barb would fly from her lips. It always calmed me.

She didn't know who the firebug was, but she knew what would happen once we reached the island: The woman would be arrested and would end up sleeping over when she'd just planned on visiting whoever was pictured in those burned photos. They had plenty of beds at Rose M. Singer, the women's jail whose name sounded like that of a former jazz chanteuse. As we crossed the bridge, I saw jets taxiing along the runways of LaGuardia Airport. On the other side of the channel was Rikers, waves lapping its rocky shores.

What I remember most vividly about my first time passing through the security checkpoints was the woman who had frisked me with a handheld metal detector. Her fingernails were so long and red, I don't know how she held the detector, much less waved it around. Those glorious talons decorated with inlaid starbursts scanned us for dangerous metal.

She let me through the security building and into the parking lot where route buses transport guards and visitors to the various jails beyond. Paige and I took a short ride to C-73, otherwise known as GMDC, where Horizon Academy was headquartered. Once we were inside, my briefcase went through a scanner and I emptied the contents of my pockets into a small plastic bucket. Just like at the airport, I thought. We passed through a set of gates into the sally port, a large space where the guards congregated, passing one another during the change of shifts.

Against one wall, a shelf of cubbyholes had been filled with riot-gear helmets and shank vests. My pulse began to accelerate while we waited near the far gate for an officer to escort us down the corridor. Finally he appeared and the gate opened, the sound of a pulley cranking link by link, peeling open a world I'd never entered awash in blues and grays. We passed a line of inmates moving in the opposite direction, men whose eyes swept over and through me, memorizing my face.

Past the library, the doors to the school corridor swung open. A long paper banner taped to one of the walls read "Welcome to Horizon Academy" in orange and green. Continuing down the hallway, we passed three classrooms on the right side and two on the left. Unlike the shouts and laughter in the barbershop, it was quiet, the scraping of pencil on paper audible. A female guard sitting at a large desk at the end of the hall whispered into a phone.

"Girl. I told her not to fuck around with Vanilla Ice. He trouble."

She paused and put down the receiver as the line approached, then pulled out a pack of Kools and shook one loose. Officer Latasha Price, from Macon, Georgia, was battle-proven. After twelve years on the island quashing riots, extracting violent felons from the cells, dousing mattress fires, and cutting suicides down from bathroom pipes, she had earned this easy post. The inmates who came down here knew not to fuck with her, just to carry their studious asses along to class and pull their baggy jeans up around their waists. She wasn't pretty, which helped, but she was also tough and loud enough to get in their chests. None of them wanted that; they'd rather see her smile and feel her warmth, reminding them of the women back home they knew better than to cross.

I had a kind of fearlessness that could pass as courage. I didn't care much about what happened to me and had few ties to anyone: estranged from my family, no girlfriend, and struggling in a new city. Not much to lose in my mind, clouded as it was by a recurrent depression I'd become intimate with, beginning with suicidal thoughts at the age of six, then again at twenty-two, and at twenty-five. Although those thoughts had quieted for several years, every time they had resurfaced they had done so more intensely. Perhaps I was unconsciously hoping this job would keep them contained, awaken some survival instinct that could protect me.

And my size intimidated: at 6'5" and 230 pounds I could inhabit space, force others to look up at me. In that way I was like many of the prisoners, bristling at any perceived encroachment, my physical size projecting an illusion that hid my fear. I was able to move in that environment with assertiveness, meeting the gaze of inmates marching down the corridors, standing tall as they passed by. At the same time, I was terrified one of them would shove me against the cement wall and stab me with a shank, the others crowding around to hide me from the guards.

We turned left from the corridor and entered the program area, a hallway with a half-dozen rooms on either side. At the end of the hallway was the school office, the words *Horizon Academy* stenciled onto a glass window. Principal Ortiz, at her desk, smiled at us as we walked in. After ushering me in, Paige excused herself and I sat down. Gloria, a short, dark-skinned woman in her forties, had a charisma and grace that were immediately apparent as she danced with the continuously shifting crises that surrounded her. She looked at me over her reading glasses, her gold bracelets and hoop earrings flashes of vitality in the otherwise subdued palette of metal desks and cinderblock walls.

We talked about the school, and it was just as Paige had promised: I could write my own curriculum and design my classes. The birth of Horizon Academy, established a mere four months previously, was sparked by an eighteen-year-old inmate who successfully sued the city, claiming he had no access to educational services. There was a school that served adolescents and another that served adults over twenty-one, but this inmate had found himself in a dead zone between eighteen and twenty-one. Horizon was specifically designed to fill this void, mandated into existence by the courts. This gave the Academy some clout but also bred resentment within the Department of Corrections because they didn't have any say in the matter. Any inmate between the ages of eighteen and twenty-one was eligible to attend classes at Horizon, which were offered five days a week from ten in the morning to four in the afternoon. Attendance was voluntary, which meant that prisoners had to line up every morning in their cell blocks to be escorted to the school area.

Impressed by my teaching experience and by Paige's recommendation, Gloria warned that this was a challenging environment. Perhaps she intuitively sensed how best to persuade me, because I responded to her warning with the usual enthusiasm I felt when presented with a challenge. When she asked me if I had any questions for her, I said I did but I'd probably just have to jump into the frying pan before I knew what they were. Gloria smiled and said, "I like you. I like your spunk. When can you start?"

She asked me to shadow Paige for a couple of days to observe her teaching. I wanted to see how she did it, how she prepared to enter one of these classrooms and engage with the inmates. As the school bell rang, we walked down the hallway.

Morning at Horizon Academy. The inmates who'd been lucky enough to make the school call had been escorted from their cells and were waiting for Paige. Lucky because they had to be ready as soon as the guards entered their cell blocks and called for them, and some guards chose to leave them behind as punishment. Once they arrived, no injury or injustice they claimed to have suffered remained unspoken as twenty of them entered the room and Paige checked them off. They nodded and looked at me as she called out their government names.

Someone thumped on the classroom door. Chewing on a toothpick, a tall white man came in and barked, "Angel Montega, you got a visitor. Get your shit together."

"Where's *my* visitor, yo? C'mon, officer, have a heart."

"Hey officer, why you interrupting our schoolin'?"

"Fuck it, I didn't wanna be here anyway. Just killin' time."

"Yeah, if Angel goes back we all goin'. You heard, officer?"

Paige turned away from the chalkboard still holding the piece of chalk she was about to write with, her face flushed.

"C'mon, guys, we have work to do today. Angel, please follow the officer."

Angel said, "Miss Paige, if I'm out, we all out."

"That's right!"

"This Horizon Academy is some bullshit. Can't even keep us in the classroom for more than five minutes."

Angel rose from his chair, and most of the students joined him, standing in the narrow rows between desks. The officer stepped out of the room and called for backup. Soon three more CO's entered the room. One yelled, "All of you, against the wall. Mandatory frisk, then you're being returned to your cells."

I looked at Paige, expecting her to say something, though she just stared at the papers on her desk. Could they do this, I thought. Take away the entire class? How could the school be run like this, when the inmates abandoned class whenever they wanted, their resolve to learn weaker than whatever drama distracted their attention or prompted their resistance to the guards? What fucked-up deal was I agreeing to?

As we left the island that day, reversing our path like crumpled machines being towed from the scene of an accident, I felt the deepest exhaustion I had ever experienced, a fatigue that extended through skin and muscle and bone, penetrating marrow and into the spirit itself. Exhaustion I would never feel anywhere else, from the inside out like a diver ascending from the depths of the ocean too quickly. On the bus seat beside me, Paige asked if I was going to keep the job. I wasn't ready to speak. She understood.

It wasn't until I climbed the steps from the subway station and emerged on 4th Street again that I felt the other part of the movement, the exhilarating rush of entering a space of almost limitless choice, breaking the surface of the water, no longer subject to its dense force of gravity. Ribs expanding, breath deepening, surrounded by scarlet coats and forest-green scarves, railings painted blue and neon pink signs glowing above open doorways. After escorting Paige to her apartment building, I strolled up Seventh

Avenue, the smell of fresh pizza wafting onto the sidewalk. As best I could, I tried to imagine doing this every day, commuting between worlds like a bird flying back to the ship with a charred twig in its beak, casting myself into the unknown and returning to the unfamiliar.

There was a wry justice at work in presenting me with this decision, a tipping of karmic scales passed from father to son. My father, a District Court judge, was known for his efforts to find creative alternatives to incarceration. He was the first judge in the country to order individuals to install breathalyzers in their cars, a distinction that landed him a brief televised appearance on *Good Morning America*. Still, he participated in a system that was inherently flawed, and I am sure he inadvertently sent more than one innocent person to prison. Now I'd been sent to teach the condemned, to risk my life in order to attend to the kind of people my father had dismissed in shackles, the strike of his gavel ringing in their ears. I'm sure many of them had cursed him and prayed for revenge. But I was coming to heal, not to harm. How would I be received? What would I be sentenced to?

I grew up, probably like most middle-class white kids, terrified of prison. Before that day with Paige, I'd never been inside one. No one in my family had ever done time. Many of my father's friends were policemen, and they'd frequently stop by the house to have a drink or to get a warrant signed. I'm sure they were the source of many of his dinnertime tales. I was too young then to perceive the razor's width of separation between lawbreakers and those who enforce the law. A few of my friends in high school had been sent away to juvenile detention, and I never saw or heard from them again. Ward was the exception that haunted me, his desire to kill obliterating his fear of consequences. I knew that there were others like him, and now I was among them. The island would school me.

Brujo

MY STUDIO IN the West Village was shrinking as I added to its sparse décor. A small table I found inlaid with cerulean blue tiles served as my desk and my dining area. A sheet of ply-board laid across cinderblocks held my stereo and Bose speakers capable of shaking the windows of the surrounding buildings. The mini-fridge below the stove burners held enough food, provided I went shopping every other day. In winter the radiator blasted such intense heat that I needed to open all of the windows, both the ones facing my table and the French doors that let out onto the fire escape.

One afternoon walking home from the island, I met one of my neighbors on the sidewalk outside my building. She was carrying a bag from the Integral Yoga health food store across the street, her unruly mane of red hair and hazel eyes contrasting with the gray cement and wintry sunlight. Our eyes met, lingered. I spoke first. Her name was Jenna, and she'd moved into the building next to mine last year after graduating from Julliard. I offered to carry her bag, the weight of it in my arms making her somehow more real, closer. I'd later learn that she read fortunes at an occult shop in the Village. If her powers of divination sensed anything that would have cautioned her from me, she must have ignored them.

Outside her door she reached for the bag, the gold ankh tattooed on the inside of her forearm peeking from her sleeve. She had a dog, a white pit bull named Brujo. When I returned a few days later after taking her to dinner, both of us shivering in our coats as we embraced, our tongues and hands searching for warmth, Brujo was waiting. He required chains, restraints, a leash, and a muzzle that resembled the face shield and shackles some inmates wore when they were transported to prevent them from spitting on guards. I waited for Jenna to enter first, then followed and let Brujo approach. He liked me and soon wanted to play, though when I felt the grip of his jaws I sensed he could easily crush my forearm. My nickname for him became "Baby Shark Mouth."

Humans weren't the problem for Brujo. Other dogs were. Any size, any shape, any breed. Most dogs when they became aggressive gave warning signs: a growl, a tensing of the muscles, hair standing on end. Not Brujo. One moment he'd sniff a dog and wag his tail, the next he'd seize the stunned animal by its throat. He would not let go. Without any feelings of animosity or fear, Brujo simply wanted to kill. Brujo was a sociopath. If he were human, he'd have owned Rikers, either as the most feared inmate or the most sadistic guard.

In order to get him to release his death grip, Jenna carried a black stick about twelve inches long. She'd try to use it to pry his jaws from around the dog's throat, but if there wasn't enough space or leverage, she had to go to plan B. Plan B was to shove the stick into Brujo's rectum. I'd wondered why one end of it was scuffed, the black paint worn off. Then Brujo would let go, not out of pain—I didn't believe he felt pain in his murderous rush—but out of surprise. The panicked owner would scowl, curse, and drag his terrified dog away.

In *The Inferno*, Cerberus the three-headed dog guards the third circle where gluttons are punished. He torments them. As Dante says, "He claws the horde of spirits, he flays and quarters them in the rain." The spirit of Virgil hurls clots of dirt into each of Cerberus's mouths and, as the beast gnaws on them, he and Dante's speaker pass by unharmed. Now I was that spirit, navigating the dangers of the island to bring something back. What did I hope to find there? And more important, what was I leaving behind other than misguided intentions and clumsy efforts to help? No, I wasn't sodomizing them with sticks; the NYPD was known to do that. I wasn't sure what I could do there, what I could offer that they would actually find useful.

Brujo was obviously not learning from Jenna's interventions. Although instinctually Brujo may have been guarding his owner, and by extension me, he also pulled us into the hell realm where he ceaselessly attacked and sought to destroy other animals weaker than he. In this way he was a four-legged version of the prisoners I'd soon teach who saw themselves as predators or prey. Which meant they'd also see me as one or the other. I'd have to choose. As a famous rapper once asked, *Where my dogs at?*

Horizon

IN THE PUBLIC eye, Rikers Island is both highly visible and completely invisible. As a concept and as an image, it resonates as a place of horrific violence and inescapable punishment, one of the last places in America that truly invoke overwhelming, universal fear. Rikers terrifies. The island's mystique shrouds its true nature from the public's gaze, that true nature being actually both more and less terrifying than is commonly believed. Our society is also complicit in this, giving scant attention to the prison scandals and stories of corruption that continually bubble to the surface. The powers in control know that once the gates are closed, Rikers is a space where social rules do not apply. The phrase I heard repeatedly: "Remember, you're in our house." And I was. Perhaps the only reliable accounts of what happens there come from former inmates who survived it, but no one listens to them. My effort is only an attempt, shaded and distorted by the words I choose and by my flawed memory.

Prisons veil; they blind the public and silence prisoners. Punishment, as Foucault famously noted, transitioned from public spectacle to private sentence. In ancient Greece, the harshest punishment was exile, because it was understood that an individual would not survive for long once removed from the community. Modern prisons embody strangely hybrid forms of exile, isolating prisoners in an unseen space where it is assumed they suffer and most often are eventually released back into a society that does not welcome them.

In 1884, New York City bought Rikers Island for $180,000. During the Civil War it had been a training ground for regiments of African American soldiers. Initially used as a prison farm, it was not until almost fifty years later that the first modern correctional facility was built on Rikers. Over time these facilities expanded and multiplied to include ten separate jails, not including the infamous barge. The prison population in the late 1990s had swelled to approximately 15,000 inmates, most of whom had not yet been sentenced or were awaiting trial. In addition, there were 7,000 correctional officers and hundreds of civilian staff members: drug counselors, physicians, social workers, legal-aid workers, and teachers. A small village, one I never imagined I would join.

At the end of the week that I spent shadowing Paige, I attended my first weekly staff meeting at Horizon Academy. After a lunch of watery green beans and a rubbery veal cutlet in the officers' mess hall, I roamed the school corridor searching for the meeting. Officer Price whistled at me and nodded her head. "They in there, Jack."

As I entered the classroom, Gloria was writing on the blackboard. I sat down at one of the battered desks and looked around at thirty other teachers and counselors in attendance. Tonya, the school social worker, saw me and smiled, one turquoise bra strap peeking out from her tight blouse. Leaning over, she gave the officer standing in the doorway a shot of cleavage before shaking out her hair and pulling it back into a ponytail. From the back of the room, a bald man wearing pink sunglasses shouted, "That's our Tonya! She's the only true professional among us! Who taught you how to maneuver in this place, baby?"

"Get the fuck out of here, Jay. Do you think I'm one of these young girls who are impressed by your bullshit talk? No one listens to you no-how. You all mouth."

"For your information, darling, I've been making babies since before you were born. You know you can't resist my charms, you sweet little *mamacita.*"

Gloria banged on a desk. "All right, Jay, settle down! Everyone, listen up!" The voices of the staff, who were ignoring her, grew louder. Finally, she pointed at a man in the front row and screamed.

"Marty! What did I just say! Are you listening! How can you be an effective teacher if you don't listen! Explain that to me!"

Chastised, Marty hunched further into his seat. He replied, "It wasn't just me, Gloria. You don't have to yell."

Gloria tossed a smirk his way and continued.

"First, I want to say that although it's been a tough week, we've increased our enrollment immensely and I'm very proud of the work you've done." They applauded. The bald man whistled.

"Now, settle down." Gloria smiled. "Regarding our program expansion, I have some bad news. I know many of you were excited about installing a weight room for the students. Although the deputy warden previously approved the project, and we've already ordered all of the equipment, the warden has now cancelled it. As some of you know, six years ago an officer was assaulted with a steel plate. The warden has decided it's too much of a security risk."

Jay cupped his hands around his mouth and booed. Others joined in.

Gloria motioned for them to quiet down. "I know it's disappointing, but there's nothing we can do about it. We have to play by D.O.C.'s rules. Remember, we're in their house."

I stared out of a barred window and tuned her out. Rules. Their house. Paige had been teaching Jean Anouilh's version of *Antigone* to her classes. As the play begins, Antigone demands that both of her brothers be buried honorably, their souls allowed to find peace. Although Polynices was strung up to rot, she defied the king's rule and buried him herself. Her father, Oedipus, had paid for disregarding the truth, for ignoring the prophecies that made divine law intelligible to mortals. She vowed not to repeat his mistake, for the gods agreed that the dead should be buried, not consigned to limbo. Eventually she was punished with death, her uncle King Creon entombing her in a cave.

Rules. But these weren't sacred laws handed down by the gods; they were lies that shifted under pressure, defeating any sense I tried to make of them. They were false promises the D.O.C. was never accountable for, words that were never transferred to official documents, words that existed only as long as the listeners chose to remember them. What else were the lives of the inmates we taught here but barely legible records, a litany of sealed files and forged signatures? When I was a kid and had written something I liked, I'd singe the edges of the paper very carefully with a match so they would turn brown and tattered. That was still the life I carried inside me, the music of special words that seemed to come from another world, one in which I could escape myself and be free.

What I didn't understand yet, couldn't have understood, was how prison education itself was a form of control. The choice was not between following divine law or the laws of man: It was all man's laws, and the way we educated the inmates played a part in enforcing these laws. We presumed to enlighten them about the need to take responsibility for their actions, to be honest with themselves about what they'd done when the state apparatus they lived inside refused to do so. Or we enlightened them about the inequities of the justice system, about structural racism and class struggle, but did not give them tools to use this knowledge, which too often only exacerbated their hostility and depression. Both alternatives made them easier to manage: They embraced responsibility and became model inmates or were predictably reactive and withdrawn. Either way, Antigone remained buried in her cave.

Queen of Cups

AFTERNOONS I ROAMED my neighborhood, enjoying the freedom of release as I emerged from the subway station and delighted in the glimmer of raindrops beading an iron lamp post, pigeons washing their wings in puddles. West of Ninth Avenue I strolled through the old industrial remnants of the Meatpacking District, glimpsing a row of carcasses strung on hooks wheeled onto the sidewalk by a man wearing a white plastic hardhat and a bloody smock. I found that the best place to buy meat was a market nearby. Inside, a curtain of thick plastic hung in front of the doorway leading to the meats, so I had to pull aside the heavy plastic sheaves as I entered, engulfed by a sub-zero blast of air so cold it made my head hurt. On the way home, carrying succulent body parts in a cheap plastic bag, I passed by an Asian transvestite who towered on stilettos as she carefully navigated the uneven cobblestones, a barbed-wire tattoo encircling her ankle.

Maybe I'd save the bones for Brujo. I was still seeing Jenna, and recently she'd agreed to give me a free reading, practicing her professional tarot card skills as we sat naked on her bed. My first card was a besieged fortress, flaming parapets and volleys of arrows whistling through smoke. My second card, the Queen of Cups. Cursed to be lost in my cups, imbibing elixirs that did not cure. Would Jenna wish to enter or to flee this burning kingdom once I'd banished the guards and sacrificed my peasantry?

She glanced at my last card, the one that would fix the others like a chemical bath sealing a photographic image. She paused, the soles of her dirty feet facing me. Then flipped it over. On the card, swinging free above the crowd, the hanged man crossed my cups and tower, my fate's script clarified. I sought escape from what my cards had revealed through her consoling touch, my hands trembling on her hips. Brujo growled in his sleep and her ankles eased over my shoulders, hooking me in.

She wanted to have unprotected sex. I refused. She was insistent, said that I could trust her. I didn't tell her I'd contracted gonorrhea from a woman who'd told me the same thing or share with her about the anxiety attacks I'd suffered in my early twenties, fearing I was infected with AIDS.

Several years earlier, when I was living in Portland, Oregon, and driving a forklift at a Doc Martens warehouse, I donated blood plasma for some extra cash. A couple of weeks later I received a letter from the Portland Health Department that I'd tested positive for either HIV or hepatitis. To find out which, I had to call the number in the letter and schedule an appointment with a counselor at the department. When I arrived, sure that I would be given a death sentence, I was told that I had tested positive for hepatitis C. A year later, after numerous repeated blood tests, I learned that the first test result had been a false positive. This reprieve struck me with the force of an intervention, and I'd vowed to be more careful.

One night in the East Village, I was drinking in a country-western bar on the edge of Tompkins Square Park and chatting with two women who came eye level to the scowling face of Ice Cube that stared from my cut-off t-shirt. Suddenly they drifted away, and a potbellied man with an Old Testament beard and Buddy Holly glasses appeared in front of me. He said I should move to the other end of the bar. Was he their father? Shaking my head, I turned back to the bar and soon heard the old man's voice again behind me shouting.

Facing him, I was surrounded by ten guys wearing leather vests. Hells Angels. Of course the old man wasn't going to go one-on-one with me, and they wouldn't fight fair. I would have been stomped into mulch, but the bouncer and the bartender jumped between us, the bouncer obviously shitting his pants as he asked them to leave and the bartender, all five feet of her, screaming at them and threatening to call the cops.

The old man took a swing at me, enraged, I believe, by the glowering face of Ice Cube, and I leaned away as his fist raked my nose. The bartender shoved him back and the bouncer grabbed me and escorted me to the door. I yelled that if I saw him again in this bar I'd kill him, and I meant it. He also shouted some threats, and he and his crew retreated out the back door.

I was furious and ashamed. Furious at what had happened, and ashamed I hadn't swung back after he'd thrown the first punch. The truth was that, surrounded by those bikers, I was scared. And I couldn't accept or forgive myself for that. A memory was triggered of my father's throwing me down two flights of stairs when I was fifteen and how I'd begged him not to hit me, his balled fist over my head. I walked a few blocks around the bar looking for them, but they were gone.

Around 2 A.M. I called Jenna, woke her up, and asked her if I could come over. I slept with her unprotected, the waves of shame welling inside me unbearable. I'd already decided I was going to return to that bar and look for the Hells Angel. A few nights later I did, walking up to the bar with a knife in my pocket. A different woman was tending bar, and I asked her if she'd seen any Hells Angels recently because I was looking for one of them. She smiled and said no, not tonight, but they'd been there the previous night and said they were looking for me.

I hadn't thought through how I was going to kill ten bikers with a pocket knife. I hadn't planned an exit strategy. I hadn't considered the irony of a teacher who instructed inmates about virtue planning to murder a member of a notorious gang in public. As I left the bar, I laughed to myself and was suddenly relieved. The pressure inside was gone. I didn't need to go back there. Despite what my cards had predicted, the angels had protected me again.

Stray Cats

I WOULDN'T HAVE called it shame then, what motivated me to return to the bar. I didn't have the words or awareness to recognize it, so quickly did it alchemize into rage. I felt as though I couldn't breathe unless I did it, as though I were possessed by an alien force that had hijacked my body. The same force that had brought many of my students to Rikers, their faces shocked with the gradual realization of where they were and what they'd done. A fast-burning fuel that left them stranded and deflated. Not the zealot's sustaining passion or the martyr's destructive indifference, but the amnesiac's self-destructive blackouts.

My third week on the island, Gloria sent me to the West Facility, an encampment of 800 beds housed inside large insulated tents called Sprungs where many inmates with communicable diseases like tuberculosis and hepatitis were held. Rigid aluminum-framed structures covered by gray plastic fabric, the Sprungs resembled huge space pods. The West Facility also contained a unit of individual cells for high-profile inmates who needed protective confinement. I would be the first instructor to ever teach in that prison, my classroom located at one end of a trailer that also housed a guard post and a legal-aid services office.

Still a stranger on the island, I was wary, unsure whether I could trust the guards and sure I couldn't trust the inmates. The only real difference between them was that they wore different uniforms. I found the program trailer and was greeted by Captain Julio Ortega, the man in charge, and Officer Johnny Lake, the officer assigned to the school area. Lake was responsible both for security in the school area and for escorting the students to and from the program trailer. He shook my hand, a smirk on his face. I handed him a list of inmates who had signed up for the school program, and he left to escort them down to class while I waited alone in the classroom.

Eventually Lake returned with ten inmates lined up in the hallway, waiting to be frisked. I'd given him a list with twenty names on it. Soon I realized that Officer Lake was not doing his job. During the first week of my class, the number of students who appeared diminished each day until only six of the twenty on my list were brought down. Gloria was not pleased. At the next weekly staff meeting, she asked me to accompany Lake as he made his school rounds to gather our students from the Sprungs.

The next morning, I asked Lake to join him on his rounds, and he growled sure, if that's what you want. He knew what I was doing, and of course he didn't like it, didn't appreciate a civilian's checking up on him. I suspected he was playing favorites during his rounds, picking up the inmates he liked or who seemed compliant and leaving behind those who gave him shit or who seemed trouble.

I walked with him along the corridors and walkways of the West Facility, my own copy of the list in hand as he told me about how the inmates could not be trusted, how the school's mission was naïve, how he'd learned the hard way after fifteen years on the job. It must have been a bracing adjustment for him to suddenly be surrounded by civilians who placed demands on him and disrupted his routine. At the same time, he had requested this position as school officer, probably because he viewed it as cushier than playing referee up in the blocks, conducting random cell searches at 4 A.M., and responding to riot alarms.

I'd never been inside a prison block before. As we walked into one of the Sprungs, the funky odor of unwashed human bodies was smothering. I was surprised to see cots aligned on the floor in rows, barely enough space between them to walk around. Many of the inmates were still sleeping, others talking quietly as they sat facing each other on their beds. Four guards were stationed on one side of the Sprung, about one guard for every twenty-five inmates. One of them took Lake's list and began circling the tent, shouting out names for the school line.

Slowly my eyes adjusted to the dim light. Figures swam toward me, an older man followed by a younger man who limped as he approached. Lake intercepted them, saying,

"You're too old, Pops. This school program is only for eighteen- to twenty-one-year-olds."

Pops replied, "Sure, okay, but I'm here to see if you all can help this young man here."

He looked at me. "He can't read or write, and I was wondering if you all can help him."

"How old is he?" I asked.

"Eigh-eighteen," the kid stuttered, drooling on his filthy sweatshirt.

I noticed he had one normal arm and a flipper in place of the other.

"Sure, come with us then," I replied, and the old man smiled and walked away.

That's how I met Gregory "Strongarm" Johnson, notorious stickup artist. Born a thalidomide baby with a damaged brain and a deformed arm, Greg was raised by gang members. The one arm he could use developed enormous strength, and somehow he learned how to coordinate one-armed robberies—though not too gracefully, I imagine, since he kept getting caught.

As we wove our way through the Sprungs, our line grew longer in rhythm with Lake's antagonism. Sneering at me, he said, "See, it takes twice as long if you wait for these guys." In the past he'd just rushed through the blocks and if guys weren't ready to immediately follow him, he'd leave them behind. Unsurprisingly, the result had been almost-empty classrooms. I encouraged him to slow down as we made our rounds, which meant we danced a lurching, awkward tango of push and pull as the growing line of inmates stumbling behind us snuck smokes, the pungent smell of menthol crawling toward us.

I had to tread a precarious line. I was there to teach the inmates, not to be Lake's friend. At the same time, he was my only protection. The inmates were testing me, seeing what they could get out of school and how they could play me. Lake was also testing, waiting for me to draw a boundary with him. Not skillful enough to manage this, I sided with the inmates and held in my anger. I could not find a position where I could relate to him without seeing him as an adversary. My class depended on his carrying out the school runs.

Walking behind him along the fenced-in walkways, I smiled whenever I spotted one of the ubiquitous stray cats slinking through tiny gaps between doors, envying their ability to find invisible spaces, to move through the points of least resistance. Black and calico, short-haired and lean, they glided through the perimeter and huddled near corners of buildings, appearing and disappearing, a reminder that some shadow of the wild persisted on the island. Every morning I joined Lake on his strolls to pick up the students, and though the tension between us grew, my class doubled, then tripled, in size.

Burning

A COMPELLING QUESTION: What is it that is confined? What can be imprisoned? Conversely, what can be released? Freed from bondage? Recently, I watched a video of the Tibetan nun Palden Choetso immolating herself in the middle of a city street to protest the Chinese government. As she stood engulfed in flame, a torch burning in her maroon robes, another Tibetan waved a white silk scarf in tribute to her sacrifice. Someone nearby filmed her on their phone, broadcasting her immolation live.

Unable to turn away, I heard Howlin' Wolf growl *I asked for water, but you gave me gasoline* and reflected on why I returned to the bar that night, how I'd been ready to risk my life when Palden Choetso had willingly sacrificed hers in the hope of liberating her people. It's one thing to not receive the thing that one has asked for, and another to douse oneself with flammable liquid and light the match. I brought the image of the burning nun again to mind, inhaled smoke fumes and rippling heat as she combusted. Exhaling, I imagined sending her cooling breezes from the Himalayas, flowing waters of mountain streams to soothe her burns. That she remained still in that space, sending compassion to her oppressors as her body burned, was inconceivable.

Her example reminded me that those who responded to the cries of the world did not linger at the threshold; they were not tourists who exploited others' pain. Instead, they voyaged to the downtown of suffering and camped out there, willing to be intimate with the hearts and minds of those they helped. Although I did not want to be anyone's martyr, I wanted to be open to the possibility of giving myself away, of wholeheartedly bearing witness and responding to what I saw. I could imagine one living that way, though I also doubted that I ever could. I was too selfish, too self-obsessed. I needed to be seen, to be acknowledged. Without that feeling, I was lost, my image of myself fractured, pieces spiraling away from one another. Deep sadness arose, the sense that I wasn't real. I'd do anything to glue those pieces back together.

As summer began, walking down the street with Jenna, holding hands and receiving compliments from passersby, felt good. Brujo had taken to me, which meant he often seized my forearms or other accessible body parts in his massive jaws and squeezed. Play bites, Jenna assured me. I rented the film *Dangerous Angels*, and we watched it together in bed, Jenna falling asleep halfway through.

The next morning she invited me on a trip with her sisters to Rockaway Beach. I'd grown up on the water, on the shores of the Chesapeake Bay in a place called Scientists' Cliffs that was founded by paleontologists in the 1930s who were drawn by the fossils preserved there. It was a pristine beach community, honeysuckle bushes spilling over the roofs of boat lockers painted green to blend in with the foliage. All of the houses had to be built with natural materials and painted in shades that blended with the surroundings.

My grandparents had a summer cabin across the street from our deck house, and my grandfather would take me out in his fifteen-foot aluminum boat, puttering across the bay to check on several crab pots that he'd kept, looking for the number written on the orange buoy marker and then pulling the slimy rope from below until the pot surfaced, dripping brine water. If there were crabs inside, he'd release the latch on the pot and shake them into a bushel basket between his legs. If not, he'd check that the fish heads he used for bait were still there, then let me throw the pot back into the water. We'd take the crabs we caught and boil them that evening. My job was to sprinkle Old Bay seasoning on their eyestalks so they wouldn't move around as much in the pot, their bluish-white claws waving blindly. My grandmother would add water to the pot and place it on the stovetop, raising the flame. Rarely, one of them would make an escape, pushing the black lid aside and clambering over the edge, falling several feet to the floor before my grandmother caught it with tongs and shoved it back into the pot, laughing. An hour later they'd be laid out on newspaper that covered our picnic table, their shells burnt orange, the color of the seasoning I'd sprinkled over them.

On our trip to Rockaway Beach, Jenna picked me up in her sister's Toyota Corolla, the other sister seated in the back with her boyfriend as I squeezed in beside him. James was massive, almost my height and fifty pounds heavier, his greased mullet pressed against the car roof. When we pulled away from the curb, I was better able to see the sisters. Cady, the older one, ranted about her and her boyfriend's latest escape from the cops, her white girl dreadlocks wound up in a dirty bandanna. The other sister, Bella, was dressed in what appeared to be rags torn from the flag of a pirate ship, a faded skull ironed onto her halter top. She and Jenna shouted at each other through most of the drive, not including the boyfriend or me in their conversation.

We stopped to buy provisions for our beach picnic. As we sped through the fluorescent aisles of the supermarket, Bella suddenly grabbed a steak and slipped it beneath her black skirt. Then the sisters began skipping together toward the checkout counters, Bella rushing past the scanners and out the door. I followed her to the parking lot and confronted her, offering to take the meat back inside and to pay for it myself. It wasn't right, stealing food when we had money to pay for it, I heard my father's voice—the judge's voice—say. Plus, how the hell were we going to cook a steak at the beach without a grill? Was she going to eat it raw? By the time we drove back to the city it would be spoiled.

She laughed at me, clutching the meat to her chest. How could I explain to her that I taught men who were paying the consequences for theft, consequences this privileged girl who had never seen a jail cell wouldn't face? That what she perceived as some kind of rebellion or resistance to authority was actually helping to sustain it, because she knew that her privilege would shield her. People who resorted to stealing food to survive didn't have this protection. What bothered me most was that I knew the meat would be wasted; it would sit in the car until we returned to the city and she threw it away. It was a stunt, a gesture without purpose, the opposite of the Tibetan nun's burning in her robes, giving herself away in an attempt to liberate all beings.

Finally, we arrived at the beach, aptly named with rocks the size of small boulders encapsulated in its pockmarked shoreline. If you ripped the orange shag carpet from the floor of a crack house, placed it outside on the pavement, and called it a lawn, it would be the equivalent of calling Rockaway shore a beach. Or dressed two crackheads in a horse suit and called it a horse.

Brujo happily chased seagulls and I imagined him returning to our tattered blankets smeared with a headdress of bloody feathers, an offering for his masters. Strewn with plastic bottles, streamers of black-green algae, and the aforementioned boulders, the shoreline appeared to have vomited on itself. Between rolling clouds, stray shafts of sunlight teased our pale, scarred flesh and reflected off the glass bottles of cheap wine one of the sisters had pulled from her satchel.

Jenna raised the bottle to her lips and took a swig. I lit a cigarette, squinting toward the waves. A silence descended, and for a few seconds it was peaceful and all seemed redeemable. Then someone shouted, the sisters singing a song and throwing sand at each other as I tasted grit in my mouth. When the sun finally began its long descent into the scummy ocean, we gathered our things and headed back to the parking lot.

On our way back to the car, we stopped by the showers housed in a concrete hut to wash off. I ducked inside the doorway, momentarily blind in the gloom of slick cement, the smell of algae and reeking piss. Cady and James entered one of the shower stalls, and Jenna and I stepped into another. Soon I heard moaning coming from the other stall, and the slap of skin on skin. Jenna reached for my face and pulled it toward hers, kissing me.

I responded, leaning away. I wasn't going to have sex with her in the shower, next to Cady and James, wasn't going to compete with their rutting noises, wasn't going to become a side note in the stories that they retold, Bella and Brujo somewhere outside listening. Months later I would venture into stalls that looked much like this one where I'd engage in sexual acts surrounded by strangers, eager to watch and be watched. Perhaps my strong aversion to Jenna's advances was my own resistance to what I really wanted. Disappointment in her eyes, Jenna turned her back to me and said it was okay. I knew that it wasn't, and I didn't care. I'd be the inhibited one, the one who wasn't cool with shoplifting, the one who barely spoke to her sisters and who hated Rockaway. I was jealous of their closeness, of their ease with one another, feeling that something inside me was broken that made me unable to respond and connect.

Eventually, the grunting in the next stall subsided and we all staggered back to the sunbaked car. Another outing in paradise, I joked, and this time no one laughed. The sisters sang show tunes the whole way back to the city, three scratchy voices caterwauling into the summer air.

Antigone

WHEN I ENTERED the classroom, they had already begun their daily journaling, writing their stories. How when it rained Darrell's spine ached where the lower vertebrae were crushed during a riot, guards clubbing him unconscious, or how Wu Kai's collarbone was snapped by a lead pipe during a fight between rival Tongs. Angel wrote about the front tooth he'd chipped falling off his bicycle, flying over his handlebars into Delancey Street and a chorus of blaring horns, scraping his palms against hot asphalt. Lamar sat beside him, not writing, his head on his desk.

"Lamar, please sit up and start your journaling."

No response.

"Lamar, if you don't feel well today, I can have the officers escort you back to your cell block. Is that what you want?"

"No."

"Then please do the assignment."

He placed his scarred hands on the desk, three cigarette burn marks between his index fingers and thumbs, and pressed himself upright. Stared at me, his eyes seething.

I waited, staring back at him. Neither of us moved. I could hear that the others had stopped writing, their stubby prison pencils no longer scratching across the blank pages.

"You can start now."

"I'm not feelin' this anymore."

Lamar stood from his desk in the back of the room, his face flushed. I stepped toward him. Everyone else was silent, the room strangely quiet in those dilating seconds as my stomach tensed, and I felt the surging cords of aggression that bound us. So this is how shit pops off, I thought, the temperature rising, vectors of rage exerting a gravitational force so powerful it warped the space around it.

Because class had just started, the door was open, and Officer Lake happened to pass by. He stood in the doorway looking at Lamar, the only inmate standing in the room, his fists clenched.

"Don't do it, Lamar. That's sixty days in the box. It ain't worth it."

I waited for Lamar to rush me, wondering if he had a weapon. I hoped he'd listen to Lake, who did not step between us. Seconds passed. I could not back down, not in front of the class. I literally could not take a step backward, my feet cemented to the floor. Lamar continued to stare at me, what I imagined were dozens of micro-calculations flickering behind his eyes.

"C'mon, son. Chill out. I'll take you back to your cell."

Suddenly, Lamar looked away from me and nodded. I walked to the other side of the room as Lake escorted him out, my heart pounding. I had to try to begin class again. My hands were shaking.

Turning my back to the students, I wrote the word *Antigone* on the board. My voice still weak, I started class again.

"Which, Antigone asks, is more moral: to follow society's codes or divine law?"

"Divine law," Darrell said. "That's the law of the most high."

"Naw, man, society's laws are what matter. Who gives a shit about divine law when society will lock you up for whatever," Wu-Kai responded.

"All I know is, teach was about to get his shit rocked."

Darrell paused. "You all right, teach? You seem a little shook."

"Yes, I'm all right. Don't worry about me. Let's get into class, okay? Want to answer the question?"

"No, not really." Laughter.

"Why, are you scared? Scared you might learn something about yourself?"

"Oh shit, he got you there! Go on, teach, tell them what's up," Wu-Kai encouraged.

"What's up is that in this play Antigone is trying to recover from the death of her two brothers. She's literally recovering Polynices' body, despite Creon's order to leave him unburied. And right now we're trying to recover from what just happened in the room a few minutes ago. You're all trying to recover from the mistakes you've made and what you've been through, which is why you chose to come to Horizon, right? How are you going to recover if you don't pay attention to what's happening in this class?"

A few heads nodded in agreement. Several others were lowered onto their desks. Did they feel that I was chastising or encouraging them? Did I want to teach them or purge myself?

"Please turn to Antigone's speech on page 45."

They flipped through the pale blue booklets on their desks. We were reading Jean Anouilh's version of the play. His *Antigone*, written during the Nazi occupation of Paris, valorized the French resistance fighters and evaded German censors by casting itself as a classical Greek tragedy whose cultural value was recognized by the Third Reich. Was I doing the same, attempting to smuggle something subversive to the students, a lyrical meditation on disobedience cloaked by its title? If so, it wasn't landing, unable to pass through the myriad disruptions and obstacles that keep the system in place. I didn't know how to communicate with these men, not really. I'd calmed down enough to walk down the rows between desks, to check that they were reading her speech. Confused, angry, tired, withdrawn—a collage of expressions swept over me as I passed by. We were together, united by the divine and human law that grappled inside us.

One thing is to see evil revealed, another is to encounter evil in one of its banal disguises, flashing white teeth and groomed hands that lure women into the cars of serial killers. I was shocked when I learned that one of my students who sat quietly in the back of the room was on trial for torturing and killing his high school English teacher, a man named Jonathan Levin. All of his students knew that Levin's family was extremely affluent, his father the chairman of Time-Warner. A popular teacher devoted to his students, Jonathan dedicated himself to teaching young people who were struggling to survive.

On May 30, 1997, my student Corey Arthur called Levin and that evening visited him at his apartment building on the Upper West Side. Arthur and his accomplice, Montoun Hart, allegedly buzzed Levin's apartment and asked if they could come up to talk. I'm sure that when he pushed the button to let his killers in, Levin never suspected the students he'd befriended intended to rob and kill him. Once inside his apartment, Arthur and Montoun duct-taped Levin to a chair, tortured him with a steak knife to obtain the code to his ATM card, and then shot him execution-style. Arthur was arrested a few days later in Brooklyn, his fingerprints found on the duct tape used to restrain Levin. While torturing Levin, the men had turned his stereo and vacuum cleaner on so the screams wouldn't be heard. I'd been teaching Corey for several months before Paige told me what he'd done. He'd said to her that I was his favorite teacher at Horizon and reminded him of his former English teacher. If you'd asked me who was the least likely killer in the room, I would have said this quiet, polite young man. The devil wears a pretty dress.

Hellfire Club

I KNEW IT was over with Jenna when one afternoon soon after our beach excursion she stepped out of the shower naked, her damp ringlets and pale curves dazzling, and I felt nothing. No attraction, just a slippery dead feeling like fishtails slapping against a block of ice, my desire gutted, tossed by gloved hands overboard. Something had changed. During that car ride back to Manhattan I'd felt erased, unseen, Jenna's closeness with her sisters obliterating me. For some reason I was humiliated by it, ashamed by what I hadn't said or done. Also, I was starting to absorb the island's trauma, what I consciously blocked out during the day, returning when I was most vulnerable. Being intimate with anyone was threatening. I began waking up at night, staring at the ceiling of the carriage house, my heart pounding, a scream trapped in my throat. Violent dreams repeated: being pushed against a wall by inmates and gutted, hands covering my mouth as the shank sliced through my dress shirt, puncturing my lungs.

Another one began with me hitchhiking on a country road at dusk. A green Pontiac GM pulled over onto the shoulder in front of me. Two black men rode in the front seat. I reached into my pocket and pulled out my wallet, checking to see how much money I had. After rifling through a bunch of ones I stumbled on a $1,000 bill. Where had I found this? Somehow, they knew about it, and that's why they'd picked me up. This was all a setup. I said I'd give them the $1,000 bill if they let me go, my hands shaking as I pulled a wad of bills from my wallet. They laughed at me. "There's no such thing as a $1,000 bill. You think we some dumb niggas, huh?" "No, I swear it's here," I said, but as I counted the bills there were only singles. "Sure, white boy," they said. "It's not your money we want."

I startled myself awake, arms outstretched, hands clawing the air above my bed. The digital alarm clock on the floor read 1 A.M. I decided to take a stroll, threw on my hoodie and jeans, and stepped into the cool night air. I needed to find something that would help me detox from the island, clear my mind. Walking several blocks toward the river, brick façades of the ancient meat warehouses shadowed by streetlights, I stumbled upon a descending staircase on the corner of 14th Street and Ninth Avenue. At the bottom, a man wearing fingerless gloves smoked a cigarette, looking bored, backlit by a red glare pulsing behind him through an open door. I was intrigued: What hidden worlds awaited me inside? Still on the edge between waking and sleep, I was also more susceptible to dreaming, more willing to enter what appeared to be a dream. I paused, then walked down the stairs, ducking past the doorman and into a vestibule where another man sat behind a counter. Behind him was a sign that read Hellfire Club. A laminated sheet listing the club rules sat on the counter. I glanced at it.

1. No alcohol or drugs permitted.
2. No touching without consent.
3. No fucking on club premises.

Where had I stumbled into? As in prison, the few rules that existed invited transgression. The man behind the counter asked for $30, which seemed like a lot of money to get into a club. I considered turning around and leaving, but I was intrigued by these rules, called by the red light leaking through the doorway behind me. I paid and walked inside, passing over a threshold into another world that would infect me with its fantasies and elicit mine.

I heard the sound of leather slapping flesh, smelled sweat and the dampness of basement walls. A long bar stretched along one wall of the first room, and on the other wall was a row of cushioned benches. As my eyes gradually adjusted, I saw three beautiful women seated on the benches, shirtless men kneeling before them sucking their toes. Another man, also seated on the bench, was watching them and furiously stroking his cock. The women looked bored, one of them meeting my eyes and staring through me as though I were transparent, an apparition or the afterimage of a camera flash. I felt simultaneously more and less real, the adrenaline rush of being caught accompanied by the sense that I was free to do whatever I liked. Some may have been repulsed, but I was thrilled. The women were professional dominatrixes, and part of their persona was to look bored when they were being serviced, but I didn't know that.

Wandering farther inside, I found the second room, a hallway flanked by rows of smaller rooms cordoned off by chains. In these stalls, various people engaged in sexual scenes while onlookers watched. Occasionally one of the watchers was invited into the scene, and then they unhooked the chain and entered the room. Again there was seeing and being seen, sexual energy passing through permeable boundaries.

I lingered in the hallway, watching the crowds rush from one stall to the next as the scenes within unfolded. In one of them, two couples were groping and kissing, switching partners back and forth and glancing at their voyeurs. Standing behind a curvaceous Latina, I reached around and grabbed her breasts, pulling her closer. She glanced up at me, smiled, and started stroking me while we watched. Inhaling the vanilla musk of her perfume, I slid my hand down her dress and she brushed it away, probably not wanting me to detect what was strapped between her legs. Most of the women at Hellfire, I soon discovered, were not women. I didn't care. I appreciated her response to my longing. Realizing I didn't have to say anything to initiate physical contact, that everyone here was waiting to be touched, I felt free to indulge myself, to act upon desires I'd learned to domesticate.

Later, I remembered in elementary school being bullied by other kids on the playground. When I'd had enough I'd grab them by their neckties and swing them around, throwing them onto the grass. One day my parents sat me down and told me they'd spoken to my teacher and that I had to stop this roughhousing. They'd never asked why I was behaving that way or whether I was defending myself. They just assumed I was at fault. Now, in Hellfire, it was as though that child had been unleashed, the one who asserted himself without holding back or being scolded.

As I wandered back to my apartment before dawn, I felt shame mixed with exhilaration. Part of the shame was conditioned by what I'd been taught about sex, and another part was the helplessness that I felt, knowing that I'd soon return to Hellfire. I was compelled by deep currents within me, ones I did not understand. One liberating element of the kink scene was that it encouraged play within roles that were freely chosen. Sub and dom, master and slave spoke to one another in the language of pain freely given and received, a language that is different for each person, as distinctive as a fingerprint in a criminal's file. My suspicion was that the roles had been chosen for me long ago, and that I was just now fathoming their intoxicating pull.

The Seagull

WIND SCULPTED THE island, rattling bus windows as we rounded a bend approaching the West Facility, barbed-wire fencing on one side, grey chop of the East River on the other. Suddenly, a large white trash bag appeared billowing from the top of the fence, shredded where it was caught in the razor wire, animated by gusts of wind. Then closer, another vision: a large seagull splayed against the fence, its wings outstretched, trapped in the wire, crucified. Eyes pecked out by its brethren, an omen, a warning clear as skulls perched on castle gates.

I could not turn away, whatever thread I spooled behind me when I entered long ago incinerated. The gull mocked me, a figure for the inmates who waited inside, cuckolded by morning light that evaporated their dreams of escape.

Most weekday mornings I joined Paige for the long commute to Rikers. It was a routine trip lightened by her stories of growing up with her alcoholic parents in a house she called "the crime scene," and of her adventures in Madagascar while she was in the Peace Corps. She was still dating my brother, a strange collision of energies, her exuberance overflowing his numbness, his withdrawal into himself another form of imprisonment she was fascinated by, probably because she imagined that she could break through and reach him. I could have warned her. My brother and I had both grown up with an alcoholic judge for a father, chaos and violence welded to absolute authority. I'd escaped, however, before he had because after my parents' divorce I'd left for college. My brother had remained behind, punished daily by my father's unpredictable rages and his demands for "quality time."

I began to miss Paige when I wasn't with her, wondering what she and my brother were doing. I pictured her holding a megaphone, shouting at him while he stared behind the glass of a soundproof booth, his voice occasionally erupting over the intercom to make corrective suggestions. I'm not sure why she persisted, why she was attracted to him other than that they'd both survived what she called the crime scene of childhood. But then so had I.

She called me to meet her outside the bagel shop near the 4th Street subway station where we grabbed our coffee and descended the stairs into an updraft of stale air and the mechanized voices announcing arrivals. Her eyes ringed with dark circles, dirty-blond hair tousled and unruly, she'd slide next to me on the orange plastic seats, our shoulders touching, and I'd smell her perfume. I never asked what she'd done the night before, as though her time with my brother didn't exist, our world these daylight wanderings below and above ground, our destination always the same island blazing in artificial light.

Once I saw her scribbling in red ink in her journal and asked her what she was writing. "Don't look, it's about your brother," she replied. I must admit I was curious about what reveries he could inspire, passions so intense they surfaced during moments of transport, demanding to be inscribed in red. And besides curiosity, what else did I feel? Competition? Envy?

She loved to talk about whatever struck her in the moment, whether the differences between us and the prison counselors who were Jesus freaks, what her brother Max told her about working for the Blue Man Group, or how many species of lemurs lived in Madagascar. Talking was the way she oriented herself, gesturing with her hands, the rhythmic pauses between sentences overrun, her speech becoming breathless. When she spoke this way it made me feel that we were the ones who were together.

When she knew I was tired of listening, she opened her journal and wrote about my brother. "Isn't red the color of correction, of do-over?" I teased. She scowled, clutching the journal to her chest. "So you do things right in front of me that you'd like to keep secret?" I asked. "How long do you think we'd be a secret?" she said. "Not long," I whispered, leaning into her until she pushed me away.

Once we were on the island I always knew where she was and how close, whether I could position myself to keep her safer to let the inmates see that I was protecting her. My hand on her waist, I spoke softly into her ear. When we taught together, she was the only woman in a room of captive men, instructing them on, among other things, the deprivation of their all-male environment, how it had shaped their uneducated desires. On the train ride back to the city that charge still hovered around her as she leaned into me, resting her head on my shoulder, our fingers entwined as I breathed the lavender smell of her hair.

Apollo Kids

SLOWLY I ACCLIMATED to Rikers, internalizing its rhythms and patterns. My daily walks with Lake into the cell blocks to retrieve my students became routine. I wasn't shocked anymore by the stench of unwashed bodies or by the faces of young men disfigured by keloid scars. I wasn't terrified when the alarms erupted and Lake pulled me to one side of the corridor as officers dressed in pads and helmets raced past. Lockdowns could occur at any time, which meant suddenly I was also confined inside prison walls, sometimes for hours.

Teaching in this environment was so impossibly absurd that I had to relax and stop resisting uncertainty. The island was controlled chaos. Even the officers were kept slightly off-balance, many of them assigned an irregular schedule referred to as the wheel. Art imitated life in the officers' mess hall, where the favorite program during mealtimes was *The Jerry Springer Show*. Scene after scene featured Steve Wilcox, that bald hulking giant, wrestling guests to the floor as another alarm sounded in the cafeteria and the riot guards ran out, preparing to beat down more inmates. The television audience clapped and hooted while I finished eating my artificial mashed potatoes and grayish veal patty.

I became better at delivering lessons with speed, engaging the students immediately in some kind of controversial argument I could then spin and weave into the discussion. Each lesson had to be self-contained, as I rarely had a consistent group of students. Because most of the inmates were awaiting trial, there was continual turnover, and I encountered an entirely different group of students every three or four months. That meant I had to establish my rapport with my students all over again and set boundaries for appropriate behavior. Paige's witty sarcasm didn't suit me. Another teacher at the George Motchan Detention Center, a Moroccan guy named Mustapha, had tried to use it, but one day a Blood named Archie had stood up from his desk and announced he was going to stab Mustapha in the heart. Wisely, Mustapha ran into the hallway and called for Officer Price.

I always told my students that I would treat them with respect and that I expected them to respect me as well. Every time I stepped into the class-room I was prepared to defend myself physically. I was aware that I may have to fight at any moment, and I believed the inmates sensed I would not hesitate.

More important than teaching academic content or skills was the act of witnessing, of listening to the men as they told their stories. Because I was one of their lifelines to the outside, I brought them cultural artifacts from the city, music and films I related to our lessons. During one class I played Ghostface Killah's latest album, *Supreme Clientele*. Over buttery horns and beats Ghostface rapped, "We Apollo kids live to spit the real." We huddled around a boom box, our heads bobbing in rhythm to the sounds bumping from the speakers. Forty-five minutes of escape inside the prison walls.

We shared many moments of joy in the classroom, listening to music together, laughing at humorous anecdotes, telling each other jokes. Moments that came from mutual empathy and an ability to create a different shared space inside prison walls. We were not only on Rikers, but we were also at Horizon Academy, free to inhabit its rooms as we wished. One afternoon when I was packing my briefcase, one of the students asked if I could stay the weekend. We laughed, but it was hard for me to leave them lined up against the wall waiting to be frisked as I walked out of the school area.

I've heard the claim that inmates, like animals, can sense primal emotions like fear and anger more acutely than other people. My experience is that many inmates possess an ability to read hidden emotions for the same reason they are master manipulators, because these skills have allowed them to survive. Criminals hone their observational abilities in the harshest envi-ronments where life can depend upon correctly interpreting a facial expres-sion or a casual glance. Often when I sensed that this was happening, that I was being read, I'd pause and reflect on what I was feeling in the moment. What were my students sensing that I couldn't see?

I brought the island with me even when I returned to the West Village, the tension I carried all day leaving me exhausted as I climbed the stairs of the subway station at West 4th Street. Beneath the tension was a rage whose source I couldn't identify. Had it been absorbed from the inmates? Was I carrying it for them, or was it my own? Did it matter? All I knew was that I'd hear someone shouting on the train or feel someone bump against me on the street and be seized by an urge to, as Archie would say, stab them through the heart. These violent fantasies were not brief; they extended in graphic detail to the point where I would chop up and dispose of the bodies. Once they began, they had to be played out in my mind to the end. There was no one I could talk to about them, but I knew I needed to do something. At night, the allure of Hellfire's smoky blaze grew stronger.

Part II

THE LABYRINTH

The Minotaur

Fall back and bump your head.
Snitches get stitches.
A buck fifty.
I be bored at night that's why I be tossing nigga's salad.
What you know about Damu?
GKB, mothafucka.
Let's go play the bathroom.
Go to the butcher and buy you some heart son.
It's on and poppin'.

RANDOM LINES OVERHEARD while the inmates were waiting in line to enter my classroom, each of them frisked, lowering their heads and pressing their hands against the gray cinderblock walls. Statements that identified the speakers' gang ties and the codes that managed prison life. Slashings were retaliation for snitching to the guards. Tossing salad was anilingus. To play the bathroom was to schedule a fight where the guards couldn't intervene.

In the myth of the Minotaur, the hero Theseus is sent to kill the beast trapped in a labyrinth. He must behead the monster, then follow the golden thread unspooled behind him back to the exit. This labyrinth, like the human brain with its 100 trillion synapses, is unbelievably complex and inescapable, shifting and adapting to the movements of those caught inside. So eventually Theseus realizes he is wandering through his own mind, is hunting his shadow self.

The South African poet and former political prisoner Breyten Breytenbach writes about the labyrinth as a metaphor for the convoluted terrain of imprisonment that is internalized. As he says, ". . . to the prisoner pushing or doing his time, the Minotaur is ultimately himself, the Mirror. And the prisoner searches for his face the way a monster dreads the looking glass." I was surrounded by these reflective surfaces during the hours I spent living with prisoners, eating their food, breathing their air.

The tunnels of my inner labyrinth multiplied. I was lost, believing in my heart that the Minotaur was me, that I was masquerading as the hero, and if anyone saw the truth they would abandon me to the punishment of the maze. The gold thread slipped from my hand. I caught walking pneumonia that lingered for months. Stacey, one of the counselors at GMDC, contracted pink eye, and as it spread, I was greeted during staff meetings by a sea of teary, reddened squints. My murderous fantasies on the subways continued, along with visions of hurling Molotov cocktails through the windows of the Hells Angels' clubhouse on East 3rd Street. I needed an escape, or at least a pause to breathe and feel what I'd become.

Day by day the labyrinth grew. I carried the prisoners' claustrophobia and need to escape, I carried the animosity between teachers and guards, I carried the physical walls and doors of Rikers, the tiered cell blocks and sally ports, the whooping alarms, the cursing shouts, the blades sleeping under tongues, the cut thread spooled on the concrete floor.

The Sweet Science

I DECIDED TO join a boxing gym to channel the aggression that had infected me and searched for one online. That's how I ended up walking into Gleason's Gym. As soon as I stepped inside its cavernous walls and heard the resounding *thwack* of gloves and the clipped whir of jump ropes, I began to relax. The warehouse space, thick with the odor of sweat, was centered on two rings where fighters sparred, shouted at by old men sporting towels over their shoulders. Bordering the rings, heavy bags and speed bags sang in different tempos, one with the bellowing thud of a bass drum, the other with a rhythmic hum tapping across the linoleum floor. The Black men in the ring swung in flurries, and when one was knocked down his trainer would yell at him until he climbed to his feet and knocked the other man down. They seemed almost superhuman to me, taking beatings to rise again and again, driven by a force inside that transcended the physical, a pure expression of will. The same force that some inmates showed, the ones who hadn't lost hope that they'd be free again.

The manager, whose name was Bruce, came over and offered to show me around, walking me through the rest of the gym's minimalist décor, no space not dedicated to some form of training. I later learned that some of the equipment was vintage: The speed bag platform had been used by Rocky Marciano. The locker room was a cement cave, naked men inside striding through clouds of steam. It was what I was looking for: spartan, without any comforts or soft corners, un-renovated and raw. No air conditioning and no heat. I followed Bruce into his office and immediately signed the membership papers, all of the injury disclaimer forms. Membership was only $35 a month, plus $15 a session if I wanted a trainer.

Bruce introduced me to my trainer, John Taliaferro. John had an ex-fighter's profile: bashed nose, scar tissue around the eyes, front teeth missing. He talked fast and moved continually, his eyes scanning the gym. He asked me what I was training for, if I just wanted to get in better shape or what? I said I wanted to learn how to fight. When could I begin sparring? John flashed his jack-o'-lantern smile, said not for a few months, we'll see how you do. I think my hubris amused him. For the next couple of months, three times a week I rode the F train into Brooklyn to train with John.

The basic routine kicked my ass: interval training of three-minute rounds followed by one minute of rest. Bells sounded in the gym to signal the beginning and end of each round. Four rounds of jumping rope to warm up, three rounds on the heavy bag, three rounds on the speed bag, three rounds inside the ring hitting the pads with John, three rounds jabbing the suspended bag, and so on for an hour and a half. John had to teach me how to throw a punch, how to move my feet, how to hold my guard. When I was in the ring, he tied my feet together with a rope to imprint the proper foot-work into my muscle memory. He told me no one should get closer to me than the length of my right arm, which I used to throw jabs. I was a southpaw, and my best punch was my left hook. I started learning various combinations: My favorite was 1-2, 1-2, 1-2, six punches led off by my right jab, all of them intended to drive my opponent across the ring and knock him out.

Soon, I bought my own gloves and hand wraps, washing them in the morning in my sink and taking them in my gym bag to Rikers. I'd toss them into the gym bag, where, clenched into damp fists, they'd ride through the underground tunnels. Jostled as I pushed my way into Dunkin's for my morning coffee and joined the crowd hustling onto the Q101, they'd finally reach the island, passing through security before I brought them into the program trailer and hung them from ceiling pipes in the frigid classroom where they steam dried and dreamt of being wound tightly around my hands that evening.

As my training sessions with John continued, I noticed he seemed more distracted. I wouldn't work very hard myself for 15 bucks a session, but I wanted to believe that he would keep challenging me, pushing me to the next level. I prodded him to let me spar in the ring. He said I wasn't quite ready yet, and he was right, though I kept asking. There were a few white girls who trained at Gleason's, and whenever they appeared John would suddenly focus on them as though he'd never seen the female form. He'd even leave our training session to go over and chat them up. Where did these girls come from? Park Slope? Williamsburg? With their long hair pulled back into ponytails, they climbed into the ring and threw punches. I talked to one of them and when she trained, she was all business, her brow furrowed in concentration as she hit the bags. I wanted to protect her; I didn't want to see her fight in the ring. Of course, she could have thought the same about me, and I wouldn't have listened to her either. She didn't need my protection any more than she needed John's attention.

Bap, bap! Bap! Bap! Bap! A drumbeat that slowly massaged the tension from my body, loosening the knots lodged in my lower abdomen, freeing up more power. That was where my punching power came from, the hips. Certain emotional trauma is stored in the hips, especially trauma associated with feeling uprooted or ungrounded, destabilized. If one imagines Rikers as a huge body lying outstretched on an island made from compacted garbage, its hips would scream with tightness. It would squint through blackened eyes at the planes taking off from LaGuardia, eager to climb to its feet but unable to move.

At Gleason's I moved constantly, jumping rope, punching, gliding in the ring. For three minutes at a time I danced; exhausted, sore, frustrated by my lack of coordination, still I kept moving, willing myself to survive until the end of the next round. During those training sessions images of the island receded, and my fists painted the bags with feverish tropical colors.

Demon Weed

AS SUMMER ARRIVED, the island began to stink. Not just the funk of unwashed bodies, which I was accustomed to, but the actual ground that reeked beneath its rotten mulch of noxious gases. While I was riding the route bus to the West Facility, the windows cracked open, my eyes would tear. The island had been a city landfill for years, had more than doubled in size as the city's trash was exiled to a place where it was forgotten. On the eve of the twenty-first century, garbage was routinely placed on barges that drifted across the seas, refused harbor at any port. At the same time, because of overcrowding, prisoners were placed on barges docked off the shores of Rikers. We sought distance from the abject, the cast away and discarded, forgetting that everything was connected, was our responsibility because it never disappeared, not completely, transformed in the shifting universe that surrounded us. They were destined to return, the tons of refuse afloat on our oceans, the human beings warehoused out of sight.

It often seemed that Horizon Academy was participating in this schizo-phrenic dance, since our efforts to rehabilitate the prisoners were consistently undermined and circumscribed by the D.O.C. We were embedded in a culture of institutionalized power, and officers frequently reminded me that I was merely a civilian. What this meant was that their authority would always trump mine, and that in the struggle between our conflicting agendas, I would always lose.

In this environment, dreams of educating and rehabilitating inmates appeared utopian if not completely naïve, the distance between what we hoped for and what we could achieve. We imagined that day when the prisoners would be released and would return to the world, but the moments they were living through seemed impenetrable. We had to journey into that darkness with them, into the gloom where all of us became invisible.

I told my students not to tell me about the charges they were facing. Once they trusted me, however, they naturally wanted to confide in me. Almost none of them claimed innocence; even those who said they were not guilty of certain crimes admitted that they had gotten away with others for years. Even though I listened, I always wished the stain those confessions left on my spirit would disappear. How did Strongarm stick up his victims with only one good arm? Why did Bison, a captain in the Bloods, shoot a cabbie in the back of the head?

Another student, Julio, offered to give me a demonstration of the skills that had landed him on Rikers. A member of the Latin Kings, Julio had a long rap sheet and had contracted HIV, he claimed, from shooting heroin. He playfully announced in class one day that he was going to take something from me before the class was over, and I wouldn't even notice it. I responded that if he touched me, I'd knock him out. I was wearing baggy jeans, with my wallet and my keys in my front pocket. During the class I circulated around the trailer room as usual, looking at student writing and helping them with small group activities. I kept my eye on Julio, catching his glances several times and jokingly shaking my fist.

As class ended and the inmates filed out of the room, Julio stopped by my desk and smiled. He reached out his hand, which held the wallet that had been in my front pocket. No one had ever picked my pocket before, much less told me beforehand that they were going to do so. Julio said since he had grown up alone on the streets as a young boy, he had perfected his technique on the city subways, lifting different objects from commuters and working his way up to wallets. I realized once such a virtuoso of thievery chose you as a target, there was no protection. Julio gave me my wallet back gently, with a smile on his face.

All magic plays with the tension between what is hidden and what is revealed. Similarly, punishment throughout the centuries has transitioned from a public spectacle to an activity concealed from view. The severity of the punishment in our contemporary penal system is directly related to the level of isolation it imposes: The most dangerous criminals are placed in super-max prisons where twenty-four-hour solitary confinement is the norm. Under recent anti-terrorism laws, political prisoners and detainees are held indefinitely in locations so secretive they are called "black sites," named because the CIA is reluctant to even acknowledge their existence. The magic show ends with the big reveal: The glamorous magician's assistant is not actually sawed in half; the white rabbit is ruffled but alive. For prisoners, though, this reveal is often dubious and anti-climactic. The rabbit has a scar between its eyes and is pissed as hell. No one wants to hire an angry rabbit for magic shows, and times have changed since the old hat trick garnered enough money to pay the bills.

The recidivism rate for Rikers is around 66 percent. Two-thirds of the prisoners who arrive there will return to its purgatorial gates and descend, step by step, into a space familiar yet also changed, refusing to conform to the pressures of memory. Memories of prison corrode in the light of freedom, like rogue software designed to erase itself once it has infected a system.

Even now, as I attempt to remember it, I am aware that my version of Rikers is marred by errors. This is not a matter of time and distance; even when I was working there, I was living inside of myself, experiencing my own particular imprisonment and chafing against the walls of my private labyrinth. There is something about the island that becomes unreal after one departs through its gates, a kind of amnesia in which the dreamer recalls, first, fragments, then nothing of the dream. How else to explain how frequently its captives return?

Though I didn't know it, I would soon be leaving the West Facility. One day Officer Lake stormed into my classroom, accompanied by two of my students who'd gone to the bathroom down the hall. I could smell the pungent odor of weed smoke filling the small program trailer.

He yelled, "These two were in the bathroom smoking weed! Everyone get your asses against the wall!"

Four other officers came into the room, and the inmates did as they were told. They were patted down as they faced the wall and were notified that they would be strip-searched. Lake told me to leave, barking at me as though I were one of the inmates. I was furious—not at Lake, whose reaction was predictable, but at the inmates who had jeopardized the school. How could they smoke this shit in the school area?

Of course, it wasn't about Horizon. These guys would have done what they did anywhere and at any time. They weren't thinking about the school when they pulled that pirated weed out of their drawers and lit it in the bathroom. They just saw an opportunity to get high and break the law. Finding such opportunities was one of their unique gifts, which is why they were in my class.

Once I saw this, I could relax and see the humor in the episode, especially in Lake's hysterical reaction and the red-eyed, smiling faces of the culprits. But it wasn't funny for long, because then Gloria said I needed to write an incident report to document my side of the story. It was the first of many such reports I wrote in order to cover my ass, as though I were a defendant whose testimony was not to be trusted. I imagined Lake writing his own incident report that countered mine, belaboring to spell *cannabis* as he squinted and pecked at the keyboard with his index fingers. I was sure Captain Ortega would proofread his report, because after what happened to Abner Louima and Amadou Diallo, city employees had learned not to free-write.

I typed my report and gave it to Gloria.

3:35 pm.—Officer Lake summons me into the hallway. He stops in front of the cracked bathroom door and asks a rhetorical question. "Smell anything? Someone's been burning ganga in the inmate bathroom."

3:45 pm.—Captain Ortega arrives on the scene. He isn't pleased. Suddenly, my students become fuckheads, a mantra he repeats while running his fingers through his receding hairline. The students are removed from my classroom, placed against a wall, and frisked. A few look over their shoulders, giving me this why am I targeted look. Because you didn't buy your drugs from the appropriate sources, I want to tell them. How do they think these officers supplement their incomes?

3:55 pm.—Lake raves "I don't want those potheads comin' down no more." I remind him that he has no evidence to prove the identity of said "heads."

3:56 pm.—Captain Ortega kicks me out of his office so he can meet with his think tank comprised of Lake and two other subordinates. Surely, they will be able to determine who burned what where when and how. I return to my classroom where all of my students suddenly appear to be likely potheads. Distracted by the commotion, they struggle to focus while I draw the structure of the cell on the board. I try an analogy: imagine if these walls were actually permeable. What do you think would flow in and out?

4:00 pm.—Captain Ortega finally emerges from his office and reads his verdict. Strip searches before and after school will be mandatory. All illegal narcotics must not only be purchased from Department of Corrections staff, but must be consumed in recreational areas approved by D.O.C. The "demon weed" and its social value should not be debated or glamorized in an educational setting. Any failure to comply with these orders is punishable with three months solitary confinement and six months of transporting drugs for approved guards.

Gloria crumpled up my report and threw it into the wastebasket beside her desk.

"What the hell is this?" she asked.

I braced myself for one of the infamous tongue-lashings I'd heard about from Paige. That week I'd already managed to piss off a couple of high-ranking guards and to lecture to a group of insanely stoned inmates about organelles.

"What is this garbage you wrote? I want to know."

"Hey, I'm sorry if . . ."

"I don't give a damn if you're sorry. Just answer me. I really want to know what the hell that was."

"I was trying to be funny. It's my way of dealing with . . ."

"Dealing? Your way, huh? I don't care about your way. You know what I gotta deal with? Irate deputy wardens who tell me about a disrespectful employee of mine who's causing friction in the school. Do you know where you are?"

I stared at the scuffed linoleum between my feet and smiled.

"You think you're funny, don't you!" Gloria screamed, picking up a stapler on her desk and slamming it down. "You're not! You better wise up before someone gets hurt. I'm not going to let you jeopardize the safety of this school."

"Whoa, calm down. I didn't have anything to do with that drug thing. If those guys manage to smuggle weed into the school area, what can I do about it?"

"Wrong, wrong, wrong. You are partially responsible. Realize this. You create a climate of antagonism that agitates the students. They see conflict between you and Lake, and they relate to you. Then they decide to act out too, because if you're acting like an immature ass, why shouldn't they as well?"

"Listen, I'm not . . ."

"No, you listen! If you want to continue to work here, you better straighten out your act. Be professional. If you have a problem with Lake, talk to me first. I'll handle it. The students look up to you, and you have to set a good example for them. I don't want to ever have this conversation with you again. I want your rewritten anecdotal report by this afternoon."

"No problem."

"Good. There better not be. Make sure you're at the staff meeting this afternoon. Goodbye."

Leaving her office, I ran into Malachai in the corridor. He'd been teaching at Horizon even longer than Paige, and like her he had done a stint in the Peace Corps. I admired his calm demeanor and the way he worked skillfully with the guards.

"So, how'd it go?" he asked.

"Jesus Christ, she doesn't let up! You can't get a word in. She just beats the shit out of you verbally."

He nodded. "We all get our turn. I've seen people come out of that office crying. Why don't we go over to the mess hall and get a bite?"

"Let's do it."

We hadn't spoken much before, but Malachai was a good listener. Wrinkles around his blue eyes and deep creases in his face suggested what he'd lived through as an old '60s radical. I'd never seen him angry, though in staff meetings he spoke passionately about what he believed in like someone who hadn't lost hope. Pushing a mess of overcooked green beans around on my plate, I finally spoke.

"I just don't know what happened. I have no clue why they would smoke that shit in school."

"Well, those guys were hiding what they were doing. I'm just glad you didn't get hurt and that no one else was injured."

"Yeah, but I should've sensed something was off."

"Maybe you did. You were in the room with twenty guys, and you couldn't do anything about what was going on down the hallway."

"I guess so. I didn't do anything."

"Listen, you did something. You watched the guards taking the students out of the bathroom, which probably saved them from a serious beating. And you kept order in the classroom. That's doing a lot."

"Thanks. I was just shocked. I didn't think they'd bring that shit down into my room. I thought they'd have more respect for what we're trying to do."

Malachai leaned back and crossed his arms, staring at me.

"Don't personalize it. It wasn't about you. They would have smoked drugs anywhere they could get away with it. They took advantage of a favorable situation without thinking about who else would be affected. They just saw an opportunity and took it."

"Yes, and they brought the wrath of Corrections down on all of us. And for what?"

"They don't care. For them, it isn't about your class. The vast majority of their lives here take place in the cell block, out of our sight. The attacks, the drug deals, the fragile gang truces and backstabbing occur around the clock. For a couple hours a day we try to connect with them and teach them something useful. Then they go back upstairs, back into the fray."

"I hear you, but it seems impossible. What the hell are we doing here, Malachai?"

"No, it's not. The situation is workable. There's a chance that on any given day a few of them may actually hear us and be ready to pull themselves out of this abyss. We've got to help them. That's what we're here for."

I pressed the heels of my hands against my eyes, dots of color flaring in the darkness.

"I'm really angry. I'm angry at them for what they did, I'm angry at the guards for abusively pounding on the guys, and I'm mad at myself for being scared. I was fucking terrified."

Malachai paused.

"That's okay. We all should be terrified. If you weren't, then I'd be worried about you. People get desensitized to the violence and the pain. That's when they get hurt, when they forget where they are and what they're doing. Remember, those guards are only half a step ahead of the inmates. Most of them come from the same neighborhoods, the same families, and have the same education. How do you think they feel about the inmates receiving the education they never did? Can you blame them for being resentful? Don't forget, we're teaching them too."

"No thanks, I'd rather not."

"Well you are whether you want to or not. Not formally so much, though sometimes a guard will sit in on one of my classes and actually seem to be paying attention. But through your interactions with them. How you treat them. How well you communicate with them. All of that matters."

"It's just too much, Malachai. I don't see how anyone could do it for very long."

"I agree. You could always go back to the Board of Ed. and get a position in one of the inner-city schools where the students don't work, the parents don't care, and the administrators could care less. At least here we have Gloria's support, and the opportunity to teach something. The inmates who are here for the right reasons work hard. I've seen how disappointed they are when one of us calls in sick or doesn't show up. They appreciate what we do."

"Not all of them."

"No, not all of them." Malachai shrugged.

"Gloria made you the school coordinator over at the prison hospital, right? How is it going?"

"Hectic. She put me in charge of our four classrooms over there. We gathered up the walking wounded and formed a student government to discuss what they wanted to learn and how we could best help them. Then our staff designed a curriculum and we've been trying to do as much as we can to get them hooked into coming down every day. Five came down yesterday. Not many, but it's a start."

"Yah, well I'm sure the CO's will strip-search all of my students tomorrow, and every day from now on probably."

"Whatever happens, we'll deal with it. Don't worry about them; that incident was beyond your reach. Just focus on teaching the best classes that you can. Your colleagues all have your back."

"I know. I guess I'll give it another shot. It's just fucking exhausting, you know?"

"Yes, I know."

I looked at Malachai as he sat perfectly still, watching me.

"Were you always this calm?"

"No way. I used to be so angry no one wanted to be around me. I had a horrible temper. I did bad things to people that I regret. Two things changed me. First, my job with the Peace Corps. Then I lost my son."

"Where were you stationed?"

"In Kenya. We built community centers. The ruling regime saw our work as a threat. I don't know why they let us into the country, probably to improve their international image. I saw a lot of killing there, whole villages terrorized, kids disemboweled and beheaded, their little skulls impaled on pikes. It opened my eyes. My own suffering didn't seem so important anymore."

"How about your son? I haven't heard you mention him before."

"It's hard for me to talk about him. He's been locked up in a federal pen in Montana for a long time now."

"Jesus, that sounds awful. Do you visit him?"

"I used to fly out there several times a year. He's prone to psychotic breaks, though, and the doctors said that after my visits he'd become so agitated they'd have to medicate him and put him in restraints. So I don't go out there as much now."

"That's terrible. Hopefully he'll get out soon."

"We'll see. Originally, he was sentenced to two to four for drug possession, but since he kept attacking the guards his sentence was extended. He's been in almost eight now."

"Can they do that?"

"Absolutely. Montana is very strict about inmate conduct, and Josh keeps racking up infractions. They don't seem to understand that he's mentally ill and can't always control himself. He may never get out."

"Sounds like they should be treating his medical condition, not punishing him for his lack of self-control."

"I agree. I've written letters to everyone I could think of: the warden, the governor, even the state senators. He's getting worse in there, not better. I think about him every day. Maybe that's part of what keeps me going here, feeling like I can make a positive change for someone else's son."

"I hope he gets out soon, I really do. And you did cheer me up, if that was what you wanted to do."

"Well, I tried. Mostly I just don't want you to quit and I want you to know that you're not alone. We all struggle in this place. In a sense, we're locked up just like they are. We have to relax into our limitations."

"I'll think about that. Thanks for the talk."

"Sure. Anytime." Malachai grabbed my orange plastic lunch tray, placed it on his own, and took them to the tray rack near the counter.

After hitting the head, I wandered up and down the school corridor searching for the weekly staff meeting. Price whistled at me and nodded her head. "They in there, Jack."

A week later I was transferred to JATC, the maximum-security prison.

Windows

WEEKDAY AFTERNOONS I climbed out of the subway tunnel and into the amber haze of city streets. First the release as my foot touched the sidewalk, and I was overwhelmed by the sense of freedom previously hidden to me, a freedom revealed only in contrast with an experience of captivity or isolation, a surging buzz that lit every molecule and cell. Even breathing felt different, as though I'd been hauled on deck after a sea dive, the heavy tank lifted from my shoulders. A little sugary rush I rode on my walk home, smiling at the office girls rushing by wearing sneakers, passing beneath chants of Hare Krishnas drifting through the open windows of the yoga studio across from my carriage house.

Sometimes I'd keep walking several blocks to the Meatpacking District, into an unmarked supermarket where I'd push aside thick plastic curtains and enter the freezing meat section, the air cold enough to burn my lungs as I selected a fresh steak to cook on my tiny stovetop. On my way back to my apartment, a faint whiff of cow shit outside the market smelled like my childhood trips to visit family in Nebraska, and I imagined the cows that supplied my steaks being slaughtered on city docks at night, blows from sledgehammers buckling their legs. I knew that wasn't true, though, because I routinely wandered these streets at all hours and saw only transvestite hookers and other insomniacs like me hoofing across the cobblestones.

Before I reached my front door, I was swallowed by paralyzing exhaustion. I hauled myself up the spiral staircase to my third-floor studio, shoved the meat into my mini-fridge, and passed out on my futon, waking in darkness, not knowing where I was.

My writing stalled. I was too wasted after a day at Rikers to attempt much, exhausted physically and emotionally. Suddenly, the practice that I had made the center of my life dissipated. It was similar to when I'd moved to Portland after finishing graduate school with a plan of working a blue-collar job during the day and writing at night. Instead, I found a temp job driving a forklift at the Doc Martens warehouse and smoked weed during my lunch breaks with some friends I'd met. Usually we lit up in the McDonald's drive-through, blowing smoke into the cashier's visor. That's what my writing process had deteriorated into: a gang of idiots in hardhats puffing on joints and screaming into a crackly voice box for fries and apple pies. The energy and focus that I needed to do my work had vanished. I felt the voices, the experiences, the images of Rikers inside me, but it would be years before I could make anything of them. I just wanted to rest and forget.

One afternoon, I peeled off my jeans and slumped in a folding chair near one of the windows in my tiny apartment. It was dusk, a soft golden light bathing the courtyard below. About twenty feet across from my window was the window of an adjacent apartment that faced mine. Sitting near his window, a man stared at me. I decided to experiment and slowly took off my t-shirt, showing the panther and snake tattooed on my arm. I looked over again and he was still staring. I began touching myself, lightly on the outside of my boxers. Glancing over, I saw him watching more intensely, his lips slightly parted as he nodded his head. Fully aroused, I slipped my boxers down and stroked myself while he watched. Above the windowsill, I could see his upper arm and elbow moving. When I came, shocks of light burst in my head as though I were pressing my fists into my eyelids. I looked over again. The watcher had disappeared.

This episode went viral in my brain. My studio was visible on both sides; the apartment windows looking into mine were occupied by others who enjoyed watching my exhibitionist show. I became the beast trapped in the maze, wandering its corridors searching to repeat the same fix. On Rikers I could be killed at any time, shanked from behind as I stood at the blackboard, my throat slit ear to ear. This was a different kind of defenselessness, the vulnerability of being compulsively locked into ritual, driven by craving. In this sense the prison followed me, pursued me as, some say, God does his chosen ones. It built a cage for me out of glass and dared me to try and escape. I could not jump inside and lock the door behind me fast enough.

I became a disembodied hand and cock, mechanically gliding with the grim determination of a doomed flying machine captured on a black-and-white film reel as it sputters ten feet above the ground and then nosedives. I was in control. Made real to myself through repetition. Pleasure centers in my brain firing, my fear and rage momentarily suspended. As Jenna had predicted, the cards of my fortune were turned over one by one, becoming darker and bloodier each passing day.

Maximum

SEVERAL MONTHS AFTER the bathroom weed fiasco, Gloria decided to move me from the West Facility to JATC, one of the maximum-security prisons. Generally, moving a teacher to a jail with a higher level of security was viewed as a promotion, a vote of confidence, but in this case I wasn't sure. Formerly the House of Detention for Men built in 1933, the James A. Thomas Center housed 1,200 inmates in individual cells. A home for hard-core criminals, not the drug-addicted burglars and stickup men of the West Facility like Strongarm, but killers and rapists waiting to be shipped upstate for lifetime bids.

The school area was deep inside the prison, a corridor with four rooms that were more like holding cells than classrooms. No windows. As I was escorted the first day to the school area, I saw a massive stone chair that looked more like a throne, molded out of a single block of gray material. Looking more closely, I noticed a small shelf with a cup that reached around the front of the chair. Each inmate, before entering school, was required to sit in that chair and place his chin on the shelf. The chair X-rayed six inches down the inmate's throat and six inches up his rectum, scanning for contraband. There would be no weed parties in the bathroom. No spitting razor blades into waiting palms.

The inmates called the main guard for the school area Panama, and he didn't take shit from anyone. Panama, like many of the guards, was ex-military, and he oozed a casual brutality as he leaned back at his desk, his feet up on a chair and a toothpick between his gold teeth. Prisoners didn't mess with him, although he seemed to expend no effort in maintaining order. Panama had the air of someone who'd kicked inmate ass for a long time and was now bored with it so he didn't need to beat someone down to get off, but he would if some newbie fucked with him. The one time I saw him become angry with an inmate who refused to obey orders, he began cursing him slowly, growling, "You punk motherfucker trying to test my shit bitch you don't know who you fucking with now you little bastard I'm gonna take you down and keep you there." The target of this verbal assault wisely focused his gaze on the glossy black surface of Panama's impeccably shined shoes, shoes whose polished tips were both threats and statements.

I couldn't get a read on Panama and I'm sure he didn't know what to make of me either, whether I was another well-intentioned Jesus freak or someone who'd sabotaged his career and had nowhere else to go. My career as such hadn't even begun and I was searching, trying to find a way through the prison of adult life where I was often confused and frustrated. I didn't have a bank account, and instead of depositing my paychecks I cashed them at a check-cashing place in Queens. I didn't take care of myself, didn't eat or dress well, and in the winter months I seemed to have a perpetual chest cold I couldn't shake. I didn't think much about my future, attempting to survive day by day in a city where every moment was effortful even for those whose psychological health was much better than mine. Panama didn't like me; he tolerated me. We both knew that eventually I was going to go somewhere else, and he was going to stay. We were in his house, which was actually the most secure wing of the larger house, the one nobody escaped from.

Although I wasn't forced to sit in the X-ray throne every time I entered the jail, I was daily scoured and examined, psychic fingers feeling down my throat and up my ass, testing whether I had the will to keep coming to a prison where teachers were not welcome by the powers in charge. JATC was a calibrated machine, and everything operated on time. If the inmates weren't in school on time, they weren't coming, and during lockdown alarms the school staff was sealed shut inside Panama's office.

It was the opposite of Foucault's panopticon: Instead of constant surveillance, nothing was visible or permitted the relief of being seen. Prisoners were trapped in smaller and smaller chambers of seclusion, culminating in solitary confinement and the madness of sense deprivation. Even insanity was not an escape since this place was built to contain it. No one needed to be seen to be monitored.

After several months Gloria asked me to visit Rose M. Singer, the women's jail, to teach a writing workshop. The only person I knew who'd taught at

Rose M. Singer was Mark, another teacher at Horizon whom I'd befriended. A former Golden Gloves champion, Mark was a tough, soft-spoken Irishman who if asked would tell about his bar-room brawls and then remove the bridge that replaced four front teeth knocked out by a sucker punch. I overheard him talking to Gloria about some outstanding criminal charge stemming from his latest bar fight. I wished I'd had him with me that night I ran into the Hells Angels. When I told him about Gloria's invitation, he relayed a story about teaching the women on Rikers.

One morning he was called to substitute for an absent teacher at Rose M. Singer. When he entered the math class, he saw that the women were already seated, their ankles bound. After a few minutes he had them engaged, helping him to answer equations he scrawled on the board. Suddenly, two women sitting next to each other began arguing about an answer. "You wrong." "No, you wrong." "Who you callin' wrong?" "You, bitch!" Since their ankles were chained, neither of them could get a good swing at the other. Instead, one of the women reached into her orange jumpsuit, pulled out a used tampon, and slapped the other woman across the face with it. Mark was stunned into silence, unable to leave his desk as the guards rushed in, the last equation on the board still unsolved.

At the staff meeting when he told this story I laughed so hard I was crying, and Gloria yelled at us for five minutes before we settled down. By that time, after almost a year at Horizon, I attended those weekly meetings wearing my sunglasses and headphones. Sitting in the back of the room with my vision and hearing occluded, I was sending the message: Please fire me. Fire me before I do something criminal and can't leave here. Enough with the bureaucratic bullshit, the disappointing news about what the D.O.C. is taking away from us now, the pressure from the New York BOE to enroll more students. I just wanted to teach, and these demoralizing information sessions were useless.

My attitude and behavior would not have been tolerated if I were the only one acting out: My colleagues interrupted the meeting constantly to throw paper at one another, shout at news they didn't like, bang their fists on their desks. We became like the inmates, our impulse control sanded down to a millimeter's width. We were childish, reactive, difficult to manage—just as they were. Unlike us, however, they were eighteen- to twenty-one-year-olds whose brains were still developing, young people who were caged in an abusive system designed to control them. Our regression was less easily explained. They were influencing us more than we were influencing them, the gravitational force of the institution sucking us under, shaping us in its image. Locked in our own parallel process, we imprisoned ourselves through over-identification with the inmates.

I glanced at Cornell, the lawyer who'd quit his firm to teach at Horizon and after six months came to work with an "X" tattooed under his left eye. For Malcom X, he'd said, his version of a teardrop. I didn't tell him that the inmates wouldn't respect him for it, that they'd just think he'd lost his fucking mind. Which he had; we all had to varying degrees. We'd been given an impossible task in a violent and dangerous setting, yet our meetings were conducted as though we were teaching in a manageable environment. We were not, and we knew it.

We laughed at Mark's story and retold it often to cope with our own fear and helplessness. We weaponized our shame, the image of that prisoner's menstrual blood smeared across the other woman's face a reminder of our own mortality. They possessed a power we would never have, and we attempted to diminish them when we spoke this way.

When I walked into Rose M. Singer, my first impression was how much cleaner it was than the men's prisons as I spotted a female inmate swabbing down the hallway floor with a rag mop. I noticed that a calmer energy pervaded the cinderblock walls, as though fewer molecules of aggression perfumed the air. I knew that most of these women were on Rikers because of some form of male stupidity or violence, that they had been objectified, beaten, hooked, pimped out, strung out, and abandoned. I was also aware that this view was limited, and as Mark's story illustrated, there were also female predators, violent offenders, and individuals who were not willing to be condescended to by being viewed as victims.

Weeks later I met them again after I stayed late on the island and had to take the last Q101 bus back to the city that evening, one filled with newly released female prisoners. Each of them hauled her possessions in a large brown paper bag as she climbed onboard, one step away from freedom. I was the only man on the bus, other than the driver. Once we drove onto the bridge, a buzz of conversation erupted, laughter and shouts and prayers and talk about who was going to do what to whom first when she hit the city.

"Girl, he know he better stop fooling with that hussy once I show up or I'm cuttin' bitches!"

"Uh huh, he better put that dick away 'cause I know you been missin' it honey."

"Shit, you better not do jack. Don't want to be right back on this bus, do you?"

"Imma sit on my front stoop and sip my wine, let the wind run up under my dress."

"Girl, you nasty."

"Whateva. All I know is I'm gonna eat the shit out of some *arroz con pollo*. No more of that raw mess hall chicken."

"I heard that. We comin' to yo' house for dinner, girl."

Sitting near the back, I had sunk into my seat and closed my eyes, hoping I was invisible. Suddenly the density of air around me shifted and I heard, "Girlllll, look who we got up in here. Think he all cute hidin' in the back."

As I opened my eyes, twenty-five heads swiveled toward me. I anticipated the whoosh of hydraulic brakes releasing as we pulled into Queens Plaza, my freshly cleaned skeleton found littering the floor, my bones smuggled offboard in those brown paper sacks.

"Wanna come party with me, handsome?" another voice inquired.

"Hey Mami, can white boy come party with us?"

"Hell yeah *amiga*."

"Come up here with us, boy. You too big to be shy."

Daring to look up at the driver's rear-view mirror, I met his gaze and caught him smiling.

Solitary

FIFTEEN STORIES TALL, the Bing housed up to 3,000 inmates who had been placed into punitive segregation. This meant a twenty-three-hour lockdown and one hour for recreation, no books, no magazines, no radios. Prisoners shouted at one another through small air vents near the ceilings of each cell. The doors were solid with a slot near the bottom for delivering meal trays. If an inmate wanted to shower, he had to approach the door and extend his hands and wrists through the slot. That narrow opening was his umbilical cord to the world outside his cell. Otherwise, he was completely encapsulated by steel and concrete, sealed inside as though he'd already been buried in his coffin.

I did not teach the prisoners confined to the Bing, though several of my colleagues did. They would sit outside a prisoner's cell and pass folders of class materials through the slot in the door. Sometimes they were greeted with urine or feces hurled through that opening, or gobs of spit and curses. Sometimes they were ignored and sat for the hour-long class waiting for the student to respond. There was no predicting what would pass through that slot, what form of communication or outrage. I dreaded being assigned there and would have refused if Gloria had asked me to volunteer. It was too close, too intimate, too cruel for me to tolerate.

I saw several of my students being transported to the Bing, dragging trash bags behind them with all of their belongings as though they were homeless and moving into a subway tunnel or bridge underpass. One of them, Darrell, looked at me and then stared at the floor as he approached me in the prison corridor. In those few seconds as we passed each other, he told me that he was going to solitary for sixty days. I didn't have time to ask him what had happened, and I knew there was nothing that I could give him, not even the promise that I would be here if and when he returned.

The cruelty of solitary confinement on Rikers has been researched and documented. Such imprisonment exacerbates mental illness and has led to numerous suicides. As a punitive method, such confinement does not have any rehabilitative value. Solitary crushes bodies and minds, a pressurized, claustrophobic space where one loses even one's own reflection. Without human contact, boundaries between inside and outside become porous, the mind subject to a corrosive deprivation.

Over days, weeks, and months, the pressure grew. Time was lost, the only indication of a world outside the small screened windows the men howled through until they lost their voices. There's no other way to say it: They were tortured. Usually torturers ask questions and extract information, but here the torture had no purpose; it was done simply to break men down, men who could do nothing to make it stop. It was a great victory that the D.O.C. was compelled to allow Horizon into this abysmal void, to let our teachers cast lifelines into its darkness, meeting with our students once a week to bring them gifts. I wish I had been strong enough to have been one of those teachers.

My off-hours became increasingly devoted to a secret life that blossomed in florid and unpredictable ways like mutated strains of hothouse flowers. I longed to be seen and touched as long as I could modulate the distance. My hunger flourished in the tight spaces between darkening panes of glass and in the subterranean stink of sweat and semen as I descended the stairs to Hellfire, its basement the Prohibition-era remnants of some illegal speakeasy or blind tiger, or exposed myself in my carriage house, another kind of solitary confinement where I was surveilled by the neighbors' windows that faced the courtyard. I was trapped, watching myself being watched. At night I wrenched open window frames that had been frequently painted over with sloppy brushes, sailors and gangsters leaning from them as they'd vomited grain alcohol onto the flagstones below.

I believe that places soak in and retain fumes of past events, attempting, as the mind does, to release trauma through repetition. I also believe in the existence of evil as a tangible presence. Before meeting this presence on Rikers, I first encountered it in a town called Eden, Ohio. I was twenty-four, on a road trip with two bisexual friends who'd paired at a mental hospital when both of them discovered they shared the same diagnosis, multiple personality disorder. We drove from Bloomington, Indiana, to Eden to visit the mother of one of them.

The most vivid image I can conjure of Saffron's mother is of her "operating" on one of her cats as it sat in her lap and she sewed a cut above its eye shut with a needle and thread. The cat was strangely compliant as I winced and looked away, staring out across miles of soybean fields dusky in the late afternoon glow. Maybe this was our earthly version of Eden, a paradise where we find ourselves held in a bony lap and whispered to while needles suture wounds we can't see, stitching us together into a single enormous beast of countless eyes and limbs.

After the successful surgery, Saffron's mother took us to an abandoned house adjoining a junkyard where she claimed she'd been abducted and held prisoner by a sadistic man. Night was approaching, so Saffron, her girlfriend Heather, and the mother all grabbed flashlights and we hopped into the car. We drove several miles to a winding dirt road that led into the promised junkyard. At the top of the hill stood a small one-floor house weathered the color and texture of elephant hide. As the last afternoon light faded, we traipsed onto the lopsided porch, the front door's rusty screen daring us to enter.

During the drive, we'd been told about how the man who'd lived there had raped her repeatedly, once blackmailing her by taking sexual pictures of her with a German shepherd and threatening to send the photos to the local newspaper if she tried to escape. She said he'd routinely kept her in the bottom of a pit into which he'd lower scraps of food and water. I realized this woman was probably insane and that her daughter had an extremely rare psychiatric disorder often triggered by pervasive childhood abuse, as well as a possible genetic factor. As we approached the junkyard I anticipated nothing more than several minutes of imaginative storytelling as I tried to be polite and mollify these women.

We peered through the flimsy screen door and stepped inside what was once the living room, an inch of dust on the floorboards. Picture the worst crime scene you can imagine: parabolas of blood sprayed across the ceiling, bloody handprints on the walls, corpses in various states of decay, their faces twisted into grimaces of anguish, their ankles and wrists scarred with rope burns. Then hastily clean it up, hose down the walls and ceiling, bag the bodies, and remove the yellow warning tape. Abandon it for six months, long enough for the elements to invade, for vermin to nest in the walls, and water to seep through cracks in the ceiling, for flocks of birds to nest in the rafters. Except they don't, since nothing living wishes to claim that space saturated with death, the house remaining in this frozen state, disheveled, desecrated, but unable to decay, to transform.

Heather and Saffron ran out of the house, saying they were freaked. They hadn't made it farther than the entryway. Maybe evil is most visible in such places, refracted by the events that occurred there as images are in a hall of mirrors. Saffron's mother told me about the abuse she'd suffered inside and how scared she'd been. I wanted to leave, but I also didn't want to abandon her as she went deeper into the house, the beams of our flashlights sweeping light over wood-paneled walls.

Suddenly she yelled, and I raced around the corner, through the kitchen to a large back room where she stood. Below, the floor of the room had been dug out into a fifteen-foot-wide, twenty-foot-deep pit that extended below the foundation. I felt an invisible kick to the chest as I gasped for air.

She said, "See, I told you. This is where he kept me and the others. You didn't believe me. See."

I wasn't listening, because whether she'd ever been there before or not, been at the bottom of that pit alone, shivering with fear, the waves of torment that radiated from that pit were palpable.

She screamed and I fell back against the doorframe, fighting an urge to run. The weak pulse of her flashlight hovered over an object at the bottom of the pit. As I looked closer, I saw a torn white cotton slip matted on the ground, soiled by dirt and who knows what else.

"I told you he took our clothes and kept us down there naked and starving," she shouted.

Again, her words were muted by the talismanic power of that slip, tossed there like the skin of some butchered animal. A trophy, a synecdoche for what had happened there. Finally, I turned and ran from the house, through the kitchen and the front room, hurtling through the screen door and almost falling off the porch. I couldn't go back inside; I didn't care if she stayed there forever shouting into the hole. I believed.

Red, White, and Blue

DURING HORIZON STAFF meetings I befriended a few colleagues. Jay was one of the veteran teachers, meaning he'd arrived several months before me. He'd worked for the past ten years at an assisted-living center for folks with disabilities, driving what he called the retard van and blasting Parliament-Funkadelic. His self-deprecating humor was one of his best qualities, and unlike most people on Rikers, he listened. This talent soon made him the choice confidant for young female counselors at Horizon who sought his advice. His incessant, predictable passes at them, like slow-motion pitches veering far from home plate, made him trustworthy in a certain predictable way. Jay later told me that one year during the Halloween parade in the Village he'd dressed up as a huge ape trapped inside a cage pulled by his drunken NYU classmates. That's how he behaved with Stacy and Tanya and Yessenia, women half his age who playfully returned his taunts, daring him to extend an arm or a leg through the bars.

We agreed to hang one afternoon after work. Jay proposed we visit one of his "secret spots" for relaxation in Queens. Thirty minutes later we were buzzed through the door of a five-story walk-up near Queens Plaza. Ascending the stairs to the third floor, Jay knocked on a large steel door.

Inside, a dozen Asian girls in bikinis sat on the floor drinking sodas and playing card games. As we entered, they crawled to their feet, lining up and sticking their chests out. An older woman, her face shaded with exhaustion, told us to pick one. Sixty dollars for a thirty-minute massage.

I'd been taken to a brothel. Most of these women were probably boat refugees, several of them of dubious legal age. Victims of sex trafficking. Jay sauntered forward and pointed to one of them in an American flag bikini, perhaps roused by her patriotic gesture, his face already flushed with anticipation. Now the madam turned to me, saying, "You pick, you pick now."

I glanced again at the floor, at candy wrappers and playing cards and soda cans strewn around. I couldn't do it. Could not pretend or justify what I knew would happen. These girls were children being held hostage. I knew what that felt like. Staring at the madam, I shrugged and said, "No, no thanks, I'll just wait downstairs."

Jay disappeared to the massage rooms with Miss America. Thirty minutes later I knew which unmarked buzzer to push, though before I reached it Jay bounded down the stairs and through the door, red-faced and smiling.

"How was it?" I asked.

"Superb, my friend, phenomenal, the full treatment."

He was flushed and panting.

"You owe me one," I said.

"Yes I do, absolutely, fear not, the love will be passed along, brother."

That's how he talked. Like an idiot burnout, a scandalous guru. And he did pay me back, in his own way.

Several weeks later we agreed to meet at the Halloween parade in the Village. As a favor, and maybe as a partial attempt to make up for the "massage parlor," he said he'd introduce me to one of his friends from NYU, a theater major who'd worked at the Playboy Club and now did play therapy with autistic children. I was wary given Jay's propensity for shameless bullshitting. Our plan was also suspect because we decided to meet on the corner of 14th Street and Fifth Avenue in what I knew would be a snarling procession of half-naked demons.

In the late nineties my cell phone resembled a sex toy purchased for its weight and girth, equipped with its own plastic holster. I refused to carry it that night but made sure I was at the corner of 14th and Fifth at the correct time, my face painted red and black, rubber horns glued to my forehead. The crush of hooting night creatures was overwhelming, hordes of fishnet thighs and wings spray-painted gold and silver, devil papier mâché puppets lofted above the crowd on broomsticks.

I floated among the stream of celebrants marching uptown, a current whose irresistible force threatened to lift me off my feet unless I yielded to it, so I had to keep circling the corner in wide arcs, returning to the spot where we were supposed to meet. Suddenly, I heard a shout, "Yo, B!" as Jay waded through the crowd dressed in an NYU sweatshirt and jeans, wearing what I realized was his most perfect costume, the aging ape dressed in his collegiate gear, the bars of his cage invisible.

Surging toward me, he embraced me in a hug and told me the same thing my mother had said for years: "When I want to find you in a crowd, I just look up." Then he said, "This is my friend Lauren, the woman I told you about," introducing me to the woman beside him dressed in ripped jeans and a peasant blouse. What had I expected, the rabbit ears and the furry tail? She reached out her hand, her flawless olive skin and blue eyes drawing me closer.

After wandering from bar to bar, jostled together as our shoulders grazed, lips almost touching, after Jay saw what was happening and grudgingly faded into the straggling crowds, we were alone, stumbling drunk into the carriage house, shedding our clothes as we climbed the spiral stairs.

The next morning, when she walked into a deli to buy bagels, patrons stared at her as she passed by a mirror and saw swaths of my red face paint smeared across her white blouse. I often joked that she'd slept with me without even having seen my face, though later I wondered if perhaps she had seen something more truthful beneath the disguise.

That was my paradise, waking in the morning next to a woman I didn't know, a stranger I'd pull close beneath the sheets, inhaling the unfamiliar smell of her skin and feeling its fleeting softness, aware I'd soon rise to make coffee in whatever morning light remained, that soon she'd dress and leave me, that I'd stretch out sated in a peaceful calm that required nothing else until the sky darkened and the familiar sense of dread returned, a self-loathing so powerful I'd do anything to escape it.

I wanted to see her again, so I called a few days later and said, "Maybe we can get together for dinner and talk and get to know each other."

"We did, don't you remember?" she replied.

A telling experiment: When given the choice between self-administering a tiny dose of heroin or a shot of the neural chemicals released during human orgasm, the mice chose the latter without exception, their hairless paws pushing the lever again and again. Hooked? More like possessed. Colonized. The gaze made flesh.

Every time I engaged in exhibitionism in my studio, every time I visited Hellfire and fondled the silk-skinned Latino she-males, every time I ventured into a booth in an adult bookstore and pushed the button that raised the screen over the clear partition, I strengthened those neural pathways. The urge to been seen strengthened, and soon I was inviting men over to my apartment, summoning the ones who peeped at me through their windows or recording invitations on gay male chatlines. I didn't question my sexuality very deeply, though I was hiding from myself and from others. My desires were limited: I didn't enjoy kissing men or touching their bodies other than their cocks. I liked jerking them off and seeing them cum, but not ass play or penetration. Mostly, I got off on dominating them, allowing men to watch me masturbate and then stopping them when they wanted to go further. Sometimes I let them touch me, but I was always in control, confident that I could beat them up and throw them out of my apartment if I needed to.

The thrill was in the choreography. A repetition of the same scene with different performers. Doubtlessly, I was working through something unconscious, attempting to master and expunge it through what psychologists call repetition compulsion. Whatever it was that drove me, the persistent sensation of being unseen and powerless, erased and without boundaries, I was sure that it also connected me with the prisoners I taught who were experiencing an exertion of force on their bodies that was largely against their will. I was perpetually imprisoned by it. There was no escape, because I carried the prison inside me.

Three nights a week I boxed at Gleason's, taking the F train to the Brooklyn Bridge. Whenever I considered skipping a training session I remembered that night with the Hells Angels and how I was scared to punch back. Then I'd unzip my gym bag, fish out my mouthguard, and bite down on it as the train left the 14th Street Station, having spared myself another descent down Hellfire's murky staircase.

Native Son

THE WORLDS I migrated through began to blur: the bliss I felt entangled with Lauren, the muscle burn and deep bone soreness after training sessions at Gleason's, and the maximum-security prison whose halogen lights exposed every jagged scar and punched-out, glaring eye socket. I transitioned between spaces, riding subway trains at every hour, scared to fall asleep and get cut by some stranger wielding a razor between his gloved fingers.

My teaching changed at JATC, and because I had a more consistent group of students attending classes, I decided to teach a novel for the first time. Usually this was impossible because each class needed to be a self-enclosed performance given that the inmates were always in flux. Without any continuity, I struggled to create a curriculum. Here, in the maximum-security prison, there was much less movement than in the Sprungs or GMDC. I could plan lessons that were cumulative and count on the same students returning to class every day. Unlike in the lesser-security jails, in this one there was virtually no other opportunity for them to leave their cells.

I chose to teach Richard Wright's novel *Native Son*. A classic protest novel that focuses on Bigger Thomas, a young Black man living on the South Side of Chicago who robs and kills a white woman, it was a controversial choice. I'm sure that if any of the guards had read it, they would have called for it to be banned. Because Gloria allowed me to choose the books that I taught, I ordered copies without asking for anyone's approval. When they arrived, I had to carry the boxes of books into the school area. Because inmates were not allowed to take the books back to their cells, we had to read them in class.

The advantage of this was that I could teach them in the moment as they were experiencing the text. The challenge was that it was slow going, and they did not have as much time to process what they were thinking and feeling, to go below the surface layer of meaning. Reading the book this way did encourage them to attend class once they were hooked into the plot.

As a teacher, I was slowly figuring out how to structure the class through trial and error. I was trying to balance different kinds of activities, group reading versus individual silent reading, short writing prompts interspersed with small group discussions, and exposure to music and visual images that illuminated the text. I hoped that the blending of these activities made the class engaging without losing the students. The consistent challenge was to adapt to the needs of students with widely divergent levels of education and ability. At least reading a common text gave us all a place to meet and to begin a conversation that could lead to deeper understanding.

The book itself was another balancing act. I chose it because when I first read it at fourteen it was one of the most powerful reading experiences of my life. It was a shocking, visceral story that immersed me in a consciousness other than my own and taught me about the power of language and the range of complex emotions that it can elicit. Although I did not like him, I had to empathize with Bigger Thomas, to suffer with him. I wanted to teach a book that the students could relate to without robbing them of the challenge of reading great literature.

Wright's novel was ambitious, an attempt to explain oppression without excusing it, to convey the malignance of racism while maintaining the possibility for social change. Some readers would say that it fails to do the latter, simply becoming a polemic that justifies violence and in doing so reduces Black men to another kind of stereotype. As James Baldwin brilliantly wrote, the novel's failure is "its insistence that it is . . . categorization alone which is real and which cannot be transcended." I wanted to honor Baldwin's damning assessment while also questioning it and placing it within the historical context in which the novel was written, a context the students could relate to because in many ways it still existed.

My attempt to teach *Native Son* was mostly a disaster. A few weeks into studying the novel, a student named Curtis yelled, "Bigger the man! He gangsta!" Other classmates responded, "Yeah, he snuffed that white woman for real!" and, "Yeah dog, but not before hittin' that pussy!" I had miscalculated. The novel was too triggering for many of the students, and they dealt with this by resorting to the kinds of simplistic readings that I wanted them to resist. From my position of privilege, as a member of Wright's intended white audience, I had viewed the character differently. For most of the students, they could see themselves portrayed in a manipulative and reductive way. On the one hand I think they appreciated Wright's attempt to communicate something that was raw and real, but on the other they felt that by assigning the book I had set them up for failure or, worse, was ridiculing them.

If I'd been seasoned and skilled enough to talk about these issues with them, the classes would have gone differently. Instead, I fell into the trap of defending the book and of giving them interpretations that I felt justified its merit. I missed the opportunity to discuss truly compelling questions about Wright's intentions and how his authorial perspective flattened the complexities of Black life, and even the question of how I saw the students from my position of privilege and power. How did the novel speak to what was occurring between us every day in these rooms? Unfortunately, I didn't have the courage or the confidence to go there, to bring the story into our shared life on the island. If the inmates reflected on these issues, they did so without my guidance. At the same time, I was slowly becoming a better teacher, improving the pacing of my class, transitioning more skillfully between activities, and seeing more of what was happening in the moment. In a technical sense, my teaching was improving, although something was missing that I longed for, an ability to connect with my students that I was searching for.

Knockdown

THREE NIGHTS A week I rode the F train across the river to DUMBO and climbed the cement stairs to Gleason's. Although I'd hoped the boxing would alleviate the violent fantasies that surfaced during my subway trips home, they actually increased in intensity as though the training were feeding on itself, seeking freedom from the confines of the ring and the gymnasium walls. I imagined razors taped to my knuckles, retractable blades extending from the toes of my combat boots as I kicked fellow passengers in the throat.

On the commute from Manhattan to Queens to Brooklyn, there was always some passenger flailing his arms and shouting obscenities, someone who careened into me as I sat crammed into an orange plastic bucket seat, someone whose madness or disregard for others called for a beating. Fighting all of them was impossible; I knew the only way to survive was to give and bend, to yield, but on a bad day I believed I could kill them all. Punching the heavy bags helped me to return, to transition between states of captivity, but it didn't take away the thirst to do damage.

Lauren enjoyed my boxing, though she swore she'd never attend one of my fights. I told her soon my face would resemble a cubist Picasso, all misplaced angles and jarring fractures. John had finally decided I was ready to spar, which meant I would be getting pummeled. I removed my contacts beforehand, which meant I was essentially half-blind in the ring. My depth perception shot, my peripheral vision compromised. This meant I couldn't see punches coming, and so my best defense was actually a hard right jab that took advantage of my long reach.

He first put me in the ring with smaller, more experienced fighters who were often able to duck under my jab, land a few body shots, and then swing for my jaw. My rhythm was jab, jab, retreat, circle, and jab. I never told John I couldn't see well and tried to compensate for what I lacked in coordination and vision with sheer aggression. Every time I entered the ring I rushed my opponent and threw the straight right-and-left combination we'd drilled over and over, attempting to knock the person out. No tentative feeling out, no jabs to calculate timing and distance, no holding back. I just swung, hoping to end the fight before my weakness was exposed.

Any experienced fighter will tell you this is a foolish strategy, a beginner's mistake. A skilled boxer will weather the initial flurry, protect himself, time the punches, and then methodically punish his exhausted opponent. I think I did manage to intimidate a few people and throw them off balance for a couple of rounds. Eventually I entered the ring with a big Mexican kid who hunkered down during my onslaught, then threw a loping right hook that landed square on my nose. Before I could register sensation, I found myself on my knees, my legs refusing to respond to signals from my brain. So this was what it felt like to be trapped inside a body that didn't listen, my thoughts screaming for me to stand up as the referee started to count.

At 5 I staggered to my feet and raised my gloves, the surprise slowly fading from my opponent's eyes. He'd caught me with a lucky shot, one that would have been easily blocked if I'd been less aggressive. I finished the round but was still dazed, my legs and arms sapped of energy. Attempting to cheer me up, John said the punch that knocked me down would have broken my nose if it had been thrown correctly.

I was devastated by the knockdown. In Lauren's apartment, I sat on the edge of her bed and stared at the floor for a couple of hours, unable to speak. I felt humiliated and defeated, my vision of catching that Hells Angel in an alley and beating him evaporated, my hopes of a perfect record in the ring gone. Did I want to continue? Could I accept being mediocre, could I face the possibility of another knockdown, of many knockdowns? Had I done enough to exorcise my ghosts?

Staring at the space between my feet, I was in a dark place, a place without words. John was an experienced trainer. He knew I needed to return to the ring soon, before the pain faded. The next morning I showed up at Gleason's on time, and in the ring waiting for me was the same Mexican with his gloves laced up, shrugging his shoulders.

Mistress Evil

ONE NIGHT AT Hellfire, a dominatrix named Mistress Evil, dressed in a leather corset and heels, leaned over the padded table and purred "Daddy," grinning at the strap in my hand. That word expelled me from my erotic dream and I dropped the strap, suddenly seeing my father's weak chin and patchy beard as he leaned across the front passenger seat of his '76 Monte Carlo to spit tobacco juice into a half-gallon plastic container. He gripped the steering wheel as the car drifted into the right lane, cutting off a red Subaru, forcing it onto the shoulder before it swerved back into the road. The driver zoomed around us, making the mistake of flipping off my father. Maybe he hadn't seen the twins Windell and Wordell, my father's steroid-crazed gym buddies, in the backseat. I was fourteen, and we'd driven to our local Gold's Gym to pump iron.

Of course the man accelerating past my father couldn't have been aware of his suicidal gesture, giving the finger to three rednecks amped up from heavy lifting, one of them the county judge. Three dangerous men flushed with testosterone and endorphins speeding along Route 2, the major highway that ran the length of the county. My father's bloodshot eyes squinted behind his aviator shades as he gunned the accelerator, tailing the conspicuous dark blue Subaru. I knew the driver wasn't a local when he turned onto a narrow road that dead-ended at the waterfront. He'd trapped himself.

I'd often seen my father lose his temper. His rage was elemental, sudden, and shocking, as when I was four or five, watching cartoons on Saturday morning and had forgotten to keep the volume down on our old rabbit-eared TV set. Suddenly, I'd feel him grab me from behind, yell, and slap me, his eyes bloodshot red, his face swollen with anger. He was enraged as though I'd done something purposely to him when I'd just gotten excited about the show I was watching and had made a mistake. After several minutes of speeding along the loose gravel road, the stranger driving the Subaru was cornered on the shoreline. I'd hoped my father would make a joke of it. Instead he gritted and bit down. Wordell and Windell squirmed in their seats, thick weight-lifting belts still cinched tight around their waists. Braking as they pulled alongside the boxed-in car, my father rolled down his window and grabbed the driver's side rear-view mirror.

The other man's face twitched as he stammered, "W. . wait a minute . . . you cut me off. . . . I almost had an accident." I saw every pore in his face, the lips moving below the hairs of his thin moustache. I didn't want to see my father hit the man. A voice I'd heard before, low and grinding, softly cursed the man. Shaking his head, he said something I didn't hear and slowly pulled away. The twins turned around and stared at the Subaru through the rear window as it sat motionless, its driver bowing his head against the steering wheel.

When I was fifteen, my father threw me down two flights of stairs in our house. I'd said something that had angered him, and he'd been drinking. After I bounced off of several walls, he knotted the collar of my shirt in one hand and drew back his fist. I begged him not to hit me. Something broke in me at that moment, something deep inside. Whatever it was, this thing urged me to destroy myself. Since I couldn't kill him, I'd kill him inside me, or at least try to as I took risks that seemed like a kind of fearlessness. Following a pimp into a crack house in Annapolis, the lights all suddenly cutting off. Driving through the projects drinking malt liquor and smoking PCP, my drug-dealing friend in the passenger seat shooting his pistol out of the car window to announce our arrival. The danger was a high I sought out, seeking the edge of what was illegal, what dwelled outside the boundaries of law, especially the law of self-preservation. For my purposes, the danger had to be real, not manufactured or staged. I had to believe in it.

Mistress Evil liked me and wanted to please me as she succumbed to the lashes, the whip raising welts on her bare thighs. She purred, and I half-heartedly struck her again. I felt the same contradictory emotions toward her as I did toward the man in the Subaru, a desire to rescue her coupled with disgust and excitement. Why was I compelled to do this, and why was she allowing me to? I could not parse her secret thoughts, read the history of her flesh, but I imagine it was very similar to mine. We were sexual criminals, deviants who reveled in filth the body could not contain, the messiness of ambiguous fluids, strong smells, delayed release of tension, moans and cries.

Many guards must have felt the same contradictory impulses when they subdued a violent inmate: sympathy for the one being overpowered coupled with an urge to dominate him. The root of what it means to be embodied is buried beneath these warring impulses, passed down through generations, encoded in our DNA and transmitted to us by our guards, our masters, our fathers.

After that first encounter, once Mistress Evil realized that I didn't want her services, the sordid rainbow of fantasy acts she was accustomed to performing at Hellfire, including foot licking, spanking, submission, golden showers, ropework, nipple torture, diapering, abduction, erotic asphyxiation, exhibitionism, teasing, needle play, rape fantasy, face slapping, fisting, double penetration, edge play, penis humiliation, and imprisonment, she was eager to talk to me. Since I didn't want anything from her, we could speak freely. I enjoyed her wit and her kindness, the thoughtful way she listened and her laughter. Initially, I tried to give her money to show that I respected her time, knowing that she'd be making a lot more if she were punishing another man instead of chatting with me, but she refused it. I never asked her for her real name, and she never asked for mine. We recognized each other beneath the words and the postures, her face still mapped in my mind. I felt protective of her, and if I entered the club and saw her in a scene in which she'd switched and was playing submissive, I'd walk away, unable to tolerate seeing her hurt even in pretend. When I had tried the submissive role once, it was she whom I allowed to hit me, feeling decibels of rage increase inside me with each lashing until I told her to stop. These sexual experiments revealed truths we often didn't wish to see. One I learned was that I reacted violently to being restrained and hit, even in play. No one was going to throw me down the stairs again; I was hurtling down them of my own volition.

I accepted her for who she was, just as she accepted me, the strange character who wanted to talk and hang out instead of play. I loved her persona, her long black hair braided with skull beads, her spiked leather collar and stiletto thigh-high boots. Nights that she was junk sick, she'd confide in me. I'd hold her hands as she made me swear that I'd never get hooked on the stuff. I promised her that I wouldn't, thinking that I also hoped to spare her from my compulsions. The same emptiness and craving drove both of us toward our separate cages, she knocking on her dealer's door after Hellfire closed and me wandering home to stare out of the darkened windows of my carriage house. Occasionally, we found each other like searchlights scouring waves at night, suddenly illuminated between the swells, the outer edges of our whirlpools touching. Mistress Evil was good to me.

Paris and Birdlegs

OUR FRIENDSHIP BEGAN with a fight after school between Paris and Eric Green, the football star who lived in my neighborhood. During the bus ride home from Calvert High, Eric and Paris must have argued about something, because suddenly word rippled down the aisle that they were going to meet in a clearing up the street from my house to settle things. I doubted Paris had much of a chance: Wiry and tall, the legs of his jeans riding around his ankles, he did not look impressive compared to Eric's bulk and his proven meanness.

Paris lived in a segregated neighborhood next to mine, marked by a turn in the road that disguised it from view. My parents always told me not to go down there, not to walk the half-mile to Parker's Creek, where Paris and his family lived. At the appointed time of the fight I was there in the field beside the bus stop, along with Eric Green and three of his friends. Why? I wasn't Eric's friend. I must have been curious. As the seconds ticked by, I almost hoped Paris wouldn't show. What chance did he have against Eric, especially coming to our neighborhood surrounded by hostile white faces? As the sun began to set, casting shadows across the asphalt road, we spotted Paris walking toward us.

He was alone. No backup, no friends. He could have been walking to a lynching. I looked into his eyes and saw fearlessness. Stepping onto the patch of grass where Eric waited, the rest of us forming a circle around them, Paris nodded his head. They clashed, grappling and falling heavily to the ground, striking with their fists. One of them would scramble to his feet and they'd collide again, throwing punches.

As the fight continued, I realized two things: one, Paris seemed to be winning, and two, Eric's friends weren't going to do anything but watch. Over and over Eric blocked Paris's fists with his face, then grabbed Paris and threw him to the ground, struggling to hold him there before he slipped free. Finally, both of them exhausted, they brushed the grass off their jeans and shook hands. I guess the fight was declared a draw, but everyone knew who had won, the kid who had dared to climb into the arena by himself, defenseless except for his hands and his heart. I'd never seen such courage.

Paris and I became friends. I walked the road to Parker's Creek after school, without my parent's permission. As I left the world I was familiar with, another arose, the sound of Black voices and R&B floating from car stereos as though the volume had been turned up. Patti LaBelle, Luther Vandross. Dirt roads instead of paved ones, shotgun cottages and clapboard houses instead of log cabins and deck houses, front yards filled with junked cars and old mattresses instead of azaleas and box gardens. A bunch of kids jumped on one of the mattresses, squealing as Paris and I sat in a junked car outside his uncle's house and he smoked Kools cigarettes.

I didn't know how he got them until I went with him to Bobby's Town & Country Liquors and saw Bobby sell him a pack. He'd never have sold them to me, even though he was old friends with my father and knew my father smoked two packs of Tareyton 100s a day. The sign next to the register clearly read "must be eighteen to buy cigarettes," but I decided that Bobby probably didn't really care about another Black kid hooked on nicotine.

In seventh grade I took a history class taught by Mrs. Rasmussen titled "Prejudice and Discrimination." Newly returned from a stint in the Peace Corps in Africa, she educated us about the American civil rights movement. A child of the '60s, she gave us a survey of the iconic images and events of that time, from the freedom riders assailed by dogs and fire hoses to the assassinations of Martin Luther King Jr. and Malcolm X. This was revolutionary material at Calverton, an all-white private school that had been established by rich white folks the year public schools were desegregated in Calvert County. After our class ended, I read *The Autobiography of Malcolm X* and Martin Luther King Jr.'s speeches. Later, I read James Foreman's autobiography and Richard Wright's memoir *Black Boy*.

The feelings of alienation and isolation, the desire for freedom, the importance of fighting for justice all resonated within me. I wanted my life to have purpose, to escape from my alcoholic household of shame and secrecy. I wanted to shed my skin, my awkward adolescent body, and become someone else. I wanted to soothe the bottomless despair that led me to first consider killing myself at the age of six, telling myself that I could make it one more year.

In later generations it became fashionable for white kids to pretend to be Black, for them to ignore their privileged position and temporarily go slumming, but long before there were white rappers or other models of cultural appropriation, I was rocking my black Adidas sweatsuit and my gold chains. The first record I owned was UTFO's "Roxanne, Roxanne"; the first cassette tape was Run-D.M.C.'s first album. I was the only white player on my school's basketball team, and most of my friends were Black. One of them gave me a nickname that stuck: Shorty Be-bop. Undoubtedly, I was confused about my identity and searching. Later in high school, I realized that my Black friends liked me much more when I wasn't trying to emulate them. But my identification with African American culture was not shallow or simple. More than merely a reaction against family dysfunction or a cry for attention, it shaped how I saw myself, how I voiced my reality. It took years for me to unravel these identifications and to discern what felt authentic beneath all of the assumed poses, to acknowledge my ability to make choices that my Black friends were never given.

I'm sure I was Paris's first white friend, as he was my first Black friend, and that we were giving each other glimpses into the other's world. I knew he'd been to Boys' Village, a detention center for adolescents, and never wanted to go there again. I also knew he was raised by his mother, and that she cared for him and his three siblings the best she could. He introduced me to his older cousin Jody, who frequently burglarized houses in my neighborhood. Had he even thought about breaking into mine? We never locked our doors, but my father kept a gun in his bedside table and slapped vanity plates on his car that read "Da Judge." I suspected Jody knew better.

After a couple of months Paris's family invited me to eat dinner with them and I was introduced to collard greens and black-eyed peas, ham hocks, and okra. Once we were done eating, we'd run outside and play basketball on the hard-packed dirt court behind their house, the hoop without a net nailed to a tree. As the last light faded from the sky, I'd hurry home, back down Parker's Creek road to my neighborhood with its deck houses and double-pane windows, passing beneath my regulation-height basketball hoop and net mounted on a fiberglass backboard. I understood that I was violating a boundary between our neighborhoods that was silently enforced so that my neighbors wouldn't need to consider what they refused to see.

His name was Robert Commodore, but everyone I knew called him Birdlegs. Every morning he traipsed the mile-and-a-half route from his unheated shack on a tobacco farm to Bobby's Town & Country Liquors. My father had given him a winter coat, which he wore this particular morning as the temperature had plunged well below freezing. His head, however, was unprotected, and finally he reached the store's warm shelter with its rows of amber bottles lined on shelves and jars of pig's knuckles on the counter. One of his friends came over, playfully reached out and grabbed his left ear. The lower half of the ear was frozen solid, and it broke off in the man's hand. Bobby's son J.P. rushed over from behind the counter and placed the partial ear in a jar in case it could be reattached. A couple of hours later, the jar was found open on the floor and the ear was missing. Either Music or Stormy, one of the two dogs who roamed the store and happily greeted customers, had gotten into the jar and eaten it.

The brutal politics of Robert's story were clearly visible: He was a Black man, living on land formerly tilled by slaves, who traveled daily to a white-owned liquor store where he was given alcohol in exchange for pumping gas outside the store. This was his only form of payment. He was enslaved not only by his addiction but also by the complicity of the store owners and the power they wielded over him. A symbiotic relationship existed between these two forms of oppression. In this sense, the loss of his ear was a physical manifestation of his immersion in a world of both self-inflicted and externally imposed silence.

What happened to Robert was not inevitable but part of a larger social construct that was extremely difficult to critique and dismantle. In my teaching, I tried to help my students to read the narrative of their lives as a story they could actively engage with and shape. They were neither powerless nor free from the oppressive forces that had guided them to Rikers. As they became conscious of their stories through hearing them echoed in the literature we studied, they felt less alone and could imagine how they could intervene in their own. Janie's determination in *Their Eyes Were Watching God* or the narrator's subversive voice in the prologue to Ellison's *Invisible Man* became models they could use to resist and endure.

The Duck Game

ON RIKERS THEY played something called the duck game. Inmates identified civilian employees who worked at the prison: counselors, teachers, clergy. They looked for someone who was vulnerable and then asked him for a favor. Something that seemed very small, like editing a letter. Later, the requests became incrementally more demanding: giving the inmate a stamp to mail the finished letter or bringing them the latest issue of their favorite magazine. Soon an invisible boundary had been crossed and what the civilian had seen as an innocuous favor, just making prisoner X's life a little more habitable, became an offense. Rules were broken, and when the inmate had enough ducks, or special favors, strung on the line he suddenly escalated his demands, asking for illegal contraband: liquor, cigarettes, porn. If the civilian refused, the inmate threatened to snitch about all of his previous favors. If he agreed, then he became a delivery boy for as long as his "friend" was incarcerated.

I thought about the children's game Duck, Duck, Goose. As long as the blackmailed civilian cooperated, he could remain a "duck," but if he refused then he was named a "goose" and was banished from the circle. There were many ways for me to be labeled a "goose": doing special favors and then refusing to be blackmailed by the inmates, infuriating guards who'd plant contraband in my briefcase and then bust me when I tried to leave, or being transferred or fired by the school administration. The opportunities for remaining a "duck," however, a person protected by the silent complicity of the circle, shrank as I penetrated the deeper layers of the prison where I was both more hidden and more intensely scrutinized.

When my compassion was ailing, I viewed men on the street asking for help as participants in the duck game who brazenly attempted to lure me into a position of compromise. "Duck, Duck, Goose," I said to myself, repeating the mantra for choosing the one who would chase us. As soon as I armed myself for a battle, my empathy fled. I had imagined that they were guilty for their lives, their circumstances, that they deserved to be locked up, shut out, silenced. True compassion did not refuse or silence. It did not distinguish between tents and mansions, beggars and kings.

Certain inmates specialized in the art of the duck game. When a man with light-green eyes complimented me on my shearling coat I did not discern his seductive tone, but when the following day he again seemed to randomly meet me outside of the entrance to the school and noted my leather briefcase, asking what books I was carrying, I felt a tremor of unease. The slightest vibration soon muffled by doubt. Was I just paranoid, hardened to kindness? So walled inside of myself that I was blind?

He left me alone for a couple of days. The next time, I saw him first, and I caught him looking for me from inside the law library. Springing into the corridor, he reached out his hand and shook mine, saying that he'd heard what a great teacher I was. In his other hand, I saw a sheaf of papers covered with black type. Thrusting them toward me, he said he was working on his appeal and asked if I'd look over his brief for grammatical mistakes. Since I was such a respected teacher, he thought, I might do this for him. A small favor. The seductive hook cast below the surface of words. The proofreading of the pages would lead to a request to send them somewhere, to smuggle them outside prison walls. What appeared to be a simple appeal would contain other code, other information that could be used by his associates on the outside. Once I'd broken that rule, he'd have leverage to make other requests. Soon I'd be a mule, my briefcase stuffed with contraband. Or not; maybe I was just paranoid and this was an opportunity to be generous to someone in need, someone who'd summoned the courage to speak to me about how I could help him. Wasn't that why I was here? I stared at him for a moment, hardened my face. "No, I can't," I said and walked away.

Part III

▓▓▓

SUBMERGED

Devil Mountain

I WAS TRANSFERRED again, this time as a reward. With Panama and the other guards at JATC, I had worked to double the number of students attending Horizon. Inside Rikers' highest-security jail, we had not had any violent incidents in the school area. I came to believe in the scanner throne that sat in the corridor, immovable as the seat of God, in its ability to morally as well as physically scour the pathways of the body. No "boofing" undetected, or slipping a razor between the cardboard slips of a matchbook. Even malicious thoughts were skimmed away, peeling off in shimmering waves of heat. We were accomplishing something for at least a few hours each day, building a kind of sanctuary inside Hell.

Gloria praised my performance and noticed that I had grown less reactive with the guards. She saw that I was able to collaborate with them without continually resenting their authority. I was offered the program coordinator position at another prison called GRVC. Coordinators supervised a team that included four other teachers and two counselors. I'd meet regularly with both the officers assigned to the school area as well as with the deputy warden to discuss how the school could be expanded while still adhering to D.O.C. procedures. And finally, I'd join the other four program coordinators who convened in Gloria's office for a weekly meeting, a kind of inner council that made policy decisions and strategized about how to implement Horizon's vision. Gloria had given me more responsibility, and I wanted to do well.

GRVC, short for the George R. Vierno Center, had 1,350 beds and housed both maximum- and medium-security inmates. Violent incidents were common: The Bloods and the Latin Kings were often at war, resulting in curfews and random searches. Our student census there was high, but whether the inmates came to Horizon for education or to recruit and communicate with gang members was uncertain. Part of my role there would be to separate the students from the hustlers.

Because GRVC was located on the far end of the island, I took a route bus past JATC and the West Facility, traveling in reverse past my former battlegrounds. We continued on a road that skirted the edges of the island, the notorious channel beyond which many escapees had drowned attempting to swim back to the city. We drove past the Vernon C. Bain prison barge. Built in 1992 from a repurposed Staten Island Ferry, the five-story ship held 800 inmates crammed into 16 dormitories. Horizon wasn't allowed to enter there, as Corrections said the security risks were too great. Images of the Middle Passage came to mind, slaves sweltering in dark, cramped holds. That barge anchored off the island wasn't going anywhere, was without course or destination.

As the bus rounded a corner, I smelled it before it came into view: a thirty-foot-high mountain of garbage rising in front of us. Composed of recyclable scraps, it stank of mildewed cardboard and wood pulp, and beneath, a richer, more nauseating odor of rotting animal flesh and eggs. A giant compost heap that seethed and belched, devouring flabby parts and soft tissue, consuming hope and vitality.

The mound was a microcosm of incarceration, the apparent stasis of captivity undercut by continuous movement and transformation. Parasitic, predatory, insatiable. Drunk maggots licking bones clean. Discarded love letters written in ink made from cigarette ash and blood fed the pile. Confiscated photos of hands flashing gang signs fed the pile. Chicken guts and feathers fed the pile. Shit-filled socks fed the pile. Buckets of grease and lye fed the pile. Nail clippings and bags of kinky hair swept from prison barbershop floors fed the pile. Semen-stained sheets knotted into ropes or nooses fed the pile. All spring the pile's fetid understory grew, its rank tendrils spreading. I began to gauge the temperature outside by the intensity of its stench.

Since ignoring the mountain was impossible, I attempted to relate to it in various ways. My first tactic was to stoically brace myself as we entered the turn, to become a stone wall. Usually I was surprised by an unanticipated scent, possibly some blood- or urine-soaked rag once dropped on the kitchen floor, its spatter drying into crusts of salt spray whose tang carried on the breeze. Some days the smell was so foul I was surprised the pile wasn't composed of the mangled bodies of inmates who'd disappeared.

Even when the mind was sealed off from the world, the imagination wandered. Another stance I took toward the mountain was that of trees whose wisdom was to bend, to be sculpted by wind. To become a lattice or a screen. This helped but was not sustainable. Fear surfaced again and drove me back into the mind of stone, of resistance. As the overwhelming stench drifted through cracked windows, I'd feel seasick and clamber back to those stone walls where at least I could feel the pain of resisting. To keep bending, keep opening to the bottomless rancid heart of the mountain, was too terrifying.

I was hungry when I finally arrived at GRVC and headed for the officers' mess hall. I carried my tray to an empty table, steam from the mystery beef stew fogging my glasses, its congealed pink lumps swimming in brown liquid not unlike what I'd seen on the mountain. Layers of noise overlapped in a cacophony: staff yelling requests to the inmate servers who ladle food onto plastic dishes, officers laughing and joking, the jangling of huge keychains as they took seats, the sporadic squawk from radios clipped to their belts, and, above all, heated arguments blasting from the TV in the corner. Always the same program was tuned in when I entered any of the officers' mess halls: *The Jerry Springer Show*. The officers cried, spitting food back onto their trays, belching and farting and hollering at the jumbled mass of bodies onscreen. Soon they'd be in it too, tackling inmates to the ground.

I glanced at my watch. Time for the school run.

My first day at GRVC, I was subbing for a science teacher who'd called in sick. As I waited for the students to arrive, I rearranged the papers on my desk, drawings of successively larger horses along with diagrams comparing the hand structures of bears, apes, and humans. Before retinal scanning or DNA our fingerprints were the markers of our identity. I thought of Che Guevara's severed hands packed in ice as evidence of his death, or the hands of American Indians hacked off by tribal police to prevent identification. My own fingerprints were locked inside a file cabinet drawer down at the Board of Education headquarters in Brooklyn. All inmates were fingerprinted under their various aliases and eventually defined by those prints, ones that confirmed their government names.

I finished writing on the chalkboard, the desks aligned neatly in rows. Staring at the back wall, I thought maybe no one would attend school today. No, they'd probably show. I waited for them in the heart of the prison, surrounded by cell blocks constructed in perfect geometric patterns.

I heard footsteps, familiar shouting.

King Lazy Eye sauntered in, limping with his cane. Twelve other inmates followed behind him, Bloods and Latin Kings. I learned later that the Kings had chosen him to lead for many reasons, the least of which was that he brought them the head of Guillermo Santiago, the Columbian hit man who'd bragged about all the pretty boys of Bogota he'd kidnapped and fucked, turning them into baby killers. Lazy Eye had challenged him to a fight in the bathroom and when it was over the shank he'd taped to his ribs was jammed into the bloody hole where Guillermo's cock had been. I remembered what the Jamaican student had told me: "Let's go play the bathroom, teach." An invitation one should most likely refuse, though I'd called his bluff and survived, guessing correctly that he was testing me.

Lazy Eye sat down slowly at a desk in the middle of the room, showing his fearlessness to those seated behind him. I read the question on the board: What is natural selection? Silence. Since none of them knew or were ready to answer, I began to explain. Twenty minutes into the lesson, as I was describing the mystery of the opposable thumb, one of the Bloods raised his hand.

"Is you sayin' we supposed to come from monkeys?" he asked suspiciously.

"Well, yes. All life forms evolve from more basic life forms. Studies suggest . . ."

"Yo, that's crazy. I don't know about you, but God made me. I ain't related to no ape." A guy next to him chimed in.

"You callin' us apes? We just savages to you? C'mon now teach."

"Yeah. My ancestors didn't swing from no damn trees and eat bananas and all that."

"Hey guys, this is just a theory. Theories should be questioned and held lightly. This theory, however, happens to have considerable evidence to support it. Charles Darwin was a scientist who was exploring what it means to be human and how all living organisms are connected through processes of natural selection and evolution."

A Muslim inmate named Jamal raised his hand.

"Sounds to me like that Darwin cat was racist, sayin' we came from monkeys and all that nonsense. That's the devilish white man's talk right there. We Five Percenters know real knowledge based on facts. Let me break it down for you. The eighty five percent consists of the devilish majority that wallows in its own ignorance. The other ten percent are peoples of African descent, the Original Man, whose mind has been trapped by false-hoods and delusion. Now check this. The black man was created in God's image. These white devils were the ones dwelling in caves like animals while our people were building magnificent civilizations. We invented writing, mathematics, science. If anyone came from apes, it's the white folks. Don't try to fool us with your tricknowledgy. It's racist and insulting."

The other students murmured in agreement. I was losing control of the room.

"Guys, guys, hold up, wait a second. I'm not trying to make you think a certain way or to impose a racist view. Jamal is right about the many accomplishments of civilizations in ancient Africa. I'm not talking about sociology or anthropology, but about biology, about the development of living organisms. The theory I'm outlining a today is one that many scholars and scientists find credible. Why? Because there's physical proof, fossilized remains and genetic data that supports it. I know that this may contradict your particular worldview or your religious beliefs, but I'm asking you to keep an open mind. Granted it isn't awe inspiring to realize we're just animals who have evolved a few steps beyond our fellow species, but it explains a lot of human behavior, doesn't it?"

"You crazy!"

"C'mon teach, ain't nothin' gonna make me believe all that!"

"Was Darwin a white man?"

"Yes, but . . ."

"Uh huh. Thought so. Well, that's a wrap."

A collective groan arose. I tried another angle.

"Hey listen, you guys are right in that some theories are sham science and are the product of deeply rooted prejudices in our society."

"Damn right!"

"And certain pseudo-scientific theories have been used to perpetuate racism."

"Speak on it teach!"

"Take phrenology, for example. Scientists claimed that by analyzing the shape of an individual's skull, certain things such as intelligence and personality traits could be determined.

"Yo, that's some devilish nonsense right there!"

"Certainly, but phrenology became quite popular around the turn of the twentieth century. Diagrams of various skull shapes and cranial abnormalities were used to diagnose patients. Individuals with low, sloping foreheads were thought to be more prone to crime."

"Yo D, what are all those dents in the back of yo knotty ass head?"

"C'mon Lamont, you know they from your mama's bedpost. She likes it rough."

"Listen nigga, don't be talkin' 'bout my mama you little gimp ass crack-head baby, or Imma give you some mo knots!"

The Muslim frowned and said, "With all due respect, teach. First you call us monkeys, and then you say that the shape of our heads proves we are criminals. Why are you trying to hoodwink us? To insult our intelligence?"

Lazy Eye suddenly spoke.

"If y'all will be quiet listen, he's trying to teach you something."

He met my eyes and nodded. The mood in the class immediately shifted. He had transferred his aura of respect to me, and I was grateful to have an ally. I passed out a timeline of the evolutionary stages of horses, the first ancestor that lived 55 million years ago barely the size of a large dog, its stout legs lengthening over centuries as it became statuesque and powerful. Eventually these majestic animals carried armored warriors into battle, hurtling across the plains toward enemies sun-struck by their glinting hooves. Riding high for the remaining forty minutes of class I swung my club, bashing the misshapen heads of unbelievers.

Island Holidays

FOURTH OF JULY. Thanksgiving. Christmas. Easter. Holidays on the island were the same as those in the free world in the sense that in both places they were sensory markers. Outside prison walls they evoked warmth and laughter, gatherings by candlelight or fireplaces conjuring ancestral memories of taking shelter by the hearth. Here, any such memories were stripped of visceral reminders, contrasting instead with rough handling by the guards, flashlight beams sweeping through cell bars, orders droned from a familiar distance.

Prison routines do not distinguish between days, months, or years. Even the harshest CO's seemed to empathize with this denial and erasure of time, as much for themselves as for the inmates. A few of them went further than the rules allowed, bringing prisoners contraband and even staging clandestine parties for them after lights out. Officer Devon Jones was busted for smuggling Hennessey into D block, while his partner Veronica Colon blew a few kingpins who later snitched her out for favorable transfers. Both of the guards were lucky that they weren't booked and sent right back to the island, returning on the other side of the bars so they could press their rookie jailers for favors.

I understood their protest against the shared depravation of spending holidays on Rikers instead of with family and loved ones. Outsiders could easily forget that even the most reviled and securely confined inmates were not alone on these days, that their captors were imprisoned with them, helping to sustain their lives at the risk of their own. All of them exiled to a place excluded from collective memory, further into the darkness than any of us would wish to go.

The despair that coursed behind prison walls fed on this feeling of being unseen and forsaken, eroding boundaries between prisoners and guards. The island wanted to turn us all into inmates, into a single collective body tortured and held captive, civilians like me willing to risk our freedom to believe that something less horrific happened there.

When a student of mine named Cole was slashed by a rival gang member as they waited in a holding cell to go to court, I visited him in the Rikers hospital, called the North Command Infirmary. He was held in the original wing, built in 1932, the same year that the U.S. Public Health Service began its forty-year Tuskegee Syphilis Study. An intern had stitched the long gash on Cole's face. He was awake and obviously in pain as I greeted him and sat beside his bed. Nearby were young men in cots who had suffered violent injuries, their flesh slashed and stabbed by sharp objects, infected by microbes, swollen and turning septic. This was not the real world where the young enjoy good health; here what was most vital was siphoned away by darker forces, sucked into a vortex where the strongest were cannibalized to feed the weakest. Cole smiled at me through the grimace of his stitches, an angry red line that ran from beside his eye to his chin.

On the day after Easter Sunday, a balmy spring morning, I rode the Q101. Outside the scratched windows, light bent against harsh angles of project brick. Faced by the scowling stares of passengers, I breathed deeply and closed my eyes, sunlight bathing the insides of my eyelids as I thought about what I could possibly give my students.

This was my job: to return again and again inside prison walls, undeterred by the blue notes of captivity wrapped inside silence. To endure the daily humiliations and eyeballing as though it were invisible and I could walk through walls. Otherwise, civilians didn't make it here, their rational minds convincing them to quit ramming their heads against immovable objects. For prisoners, the opposite movement was just as impossible to sustain—the will to get out jail and stay out, to remove the institutional hardwiring laced deep within their minds and bodies. Something I could never do for them.

Gloria called to tell me to expect a visit from Ironhorse, a theater group based in Manhattan that wanted to teach a workshop at Horizon. Since we'd finished *Antigone*, I thought the students would be receptive to doing a dramatic reading of a few scenes from a more contemporary play, learning its structure from the inside out. To survive on the island they acted constantly, performing roles and abandoning them with an understanding that they'd be left here, that the rouged and lip-glossed femme fatales, the commissary extortionists, and born-again preachers were apparitions of their public selves, hidden beneath other personae like scented handkerchiefs tucked inside boxers. They showed themselves as they wanted to be perceived, and I did the same, concealing my secret life in West Village basements and inside carriage house walls.

One afternoon not long after Gloria's message, two men arrived from Ironhorse, tall white men with close-cropped graying hair and glasses. Greg and Franz, co-founders of the company, had arrived to introduce themselves to the students and lead them in a theater class. I'd already prepped the guys and had threatened to rescind their basketball privileges for the month if they misbehaved. Franz explained that their group practiced improvisation, a spontaneous performance of action through space that was based on interactions between participants.

I started to sweat, a tightness gripping my chest. Gloria hadn't told me that this was an improv group. I'd naïvely assumed that Ironhorse would be staging written scenes, not attempting to create them in the moment. The inmates needed more structure, more direction than to be told to act like a shirt blown off the branch of a tree. Staring at Franz as he continued to explain the process, I thought, he doesn't know where he is or whom he is talking to. There was no safety here, no limits or boundaries that did not need to be continually reinforced, re-inscribed into prisoners' bodies through processes that I mostly had not seen. This was not the venue for untethering impulse from reflection. If they had truly empathized with these men, they would have supported the boundaries that were in place rather than tried to destroy them. My role was simply to make sure that the students didn't pull down their sweatpants and start jacking off as these white guys spoke to them about using their imaginations. So far, it was going well.

Greg asked the inmates to stand up. Grudgingly they did, more bemused than annoyed as they pulled up their pants and stood in front of their desks. Franz directed them to form a circle and called for two volunteers to join him in the center. No one moved. Franz waited. Nothing. Eventually he looked at me as though I were the co-director of this charade. I didn't give a damn if anyone participated or not, but I knew that none of them wanted to be the ones who volunteered to turn their backs to everyone else in the circle. Franz said he would demonstrate the exercise first with Greg, and as they stood together inside the circle he said, "Imagine you're picking up an object and handing it to your partner. Then your partner has to modify the object in some way and pass it back to you. Then you have to do something with it. Got it? It's easy."

He bent down and pretended to pick up something off the floor, stretched it between his fingers as though it were elastic, and handed it to Greg. Greg held it up, appearing puzzled, and then brought one end of it to his lips, blowing hard as it inflated, his extended hand shaping the balloon. He then tied off the imaginary sphere and gave it back to Franz, who smiled and punched it up into the air.

They called for volunteers again. Who wanted to play the game now? Silence. Greg and Franz stared at each other, grimacing. Fuck it, something had to happen. I said, "Talib and Menace, come on up. It's your turn on stage. If you want to play ball with us later, you'll participate."

They looked at me and shook their heads, ambling into the center of the circle.

Franz told Talib to go first, unaware that he despised Menace and suspected that he and the other Bloods had been trying to punk the Muslim students. Talib reached toward the floor and sprang up, raised his arm and pointed at Menace's jutting brow, his hand shaped like a gun. Simultaneously he mimicked the sound of gunfire, shouting, "Bdap bdap bdap! Take that, nigga! Three to the dome!"

Menace rocked back on his heels and frowned. Franz stepped between them, encouraged by what he didn't understand.

He said, "All right, okay, now put it down on the floor and let your partner pick it up. Remember, you're transforming the object into something else, something of your own."

Talib tossed the imaginary object at Menace's feet. He bent down and picked it up with his thumb and forefinger, raising it to his lips and taking an imaginary drag.

"Ah, this chronic is the shit!" he exclaimed, leaning toward Talib and blowing unseen smoke in his face, spraying him with a mist of saliva.

He said, "Y'all Meccafied niggas don't know nothin' 'bout this shit here! Hey Lazy Eye, wanna hit off this dog?"

Talib stepped forward past Franz and bumped chests with Menace. Franz and Greg glanced at me as though seeking my approval. In seconds the whole class would erupt in a brawl while they ran out of the room. I grabbed Menace's shoulder before he could retaliate and guided him away from the center.

Greg took charge next, ready for round two of their object exercise. Lupe and Flavio volunteered, encouraged by the last round of gunplay and blunts. They argued over who would go first.

Lupe said, "Yo, Flavio, let me set it off, I got a good idea."

Flavio urged, "Yo, me too, Lupe! I got some real Colombian shit waiting over here that's going to put that garbage weed to shame."

Lupe bent his knees and pretended to pick up something heavy. Holding his catch in an empty bear hug, he ground his hips in the air and grunted.

"What are you doing?" Greg asked.

Lupe smiled, "I'm fucking my old lady, you *maricon*. You didn't say the object couldn't be alive, right?"

All the Kings hooted and cheered. Lupe speed-fucked his make-believe girlfriend from behind, pulling her hair and cursing.

Greg yelled, "All right, enough! Guys, I don't want to stifle your creativity, but you need to be serious. Let's focus now. Use your imagination. The object may not be one you've seen before, it may be completely outside of the realm of your experience, like a huge icicle in the middle of July."

Lupe dropped his imaginary girlfriend on the floor. Then Flavio reached down and picked something up, pulling it from the floor hand over hand, whatever it was at least twenty feet long. Seeming to lose control of it, he leaned back and pretended to reel it in.

He pointed at Lupe and said, "You smell that. I bet you do. I bet you can even taste it, right?"

"What's that?" Lupe asked.

"That's my *pinga* in your mouth, nigga. It smells like your girl's chocha, 'cause I been fuckin' her for you, bro!"

Lupe pretended to smack him and they tussled, suddenly rolling on the floor. Exasperated, Greg stamped his foot.

"Stop playing around, guys! We should be taking this seriously. It's not only about guns and drugs and chicks!"

Greg winced when he said "chicks," the word mangled by his heavy German accent so it sounded like "chucks."

Flavio protested, "You didn't say nothin' about no gats or trees or nothin' else. We usin' what we imagine, what we criminals think about. What about you? You think about girls or what?"

"Sometimes," Greg responded, "but that doesn't matter."

Lupe interrupted, "Naw, I think you think about men, don't you? Yo, you can tell us."

"Yah," Flavio chimed in, "I bet you *maricon*, right? You theater dudes are suspect." Again, Greg and Franz looked at me as though I'd invited them here.

I knew what they wanted me to do, so I said, "All right guys, now keep your mouths shut and show some respect for our guests. This isn't playtime, and I expect all of you to cooperate. If you have a problem doing that, or you decide that you don't want to participate in the theater project, then you can leave and go back to your cells."

"Ah shit, Teach, you don't have to take it there!"

"Yeah, we was just playin' these fools!"

I turned to Franz. "How 'bout we end for today? Thank you for bringing something original to these guys. I'm sure they will remember it."

I wanted to get them out of there before they started something that I couldn't stop. The inmates could barely sit still after being triggered by acting out these fantasies, ones that weren't truly their own but had been imposed upon them, leading back to the original fantasy brought in by Ironhorse that they'd perform for them, put on a show that would validate what Franz and Greg imagined they were doing. "Exploitation" was another word for it. The same game that kept these men incarcerated, sold under the guise of art.

Redpath

A FEW WEEKS later, a teacher visited my classroom who would change my life. His name was Dr. Redpath, a former professor at St. John's University who was volunteering to teach at Horizon twice a week. A philosopher, he was committed to inquiry, to asking questions without answers. Although I was stunned by his methods, he transformed the way that I taught. Initially I thought he seemed lost, wearing his baggy suits every day despite the temperature and walking into class without any books or notes. In his early sixties, he looked like a former professor who after a traumatic divorce or a stint in rehab had found himself here, washed up on the island.

The first day he guest-taught my class, he passed out packets of stapled papers. When I asked if the students needed pencils or their journals, he said no. Suddenly, he began to question the students, asking, "What is justice? How can it be defined?" And he waited, at least thirty seconds, before someone responded. Then he asked another question: "Is the meaning of justice to help your friends and to harm your enemies?" Everyone in class agreed that it was; it was the central tenet of the gang tribalism they followed. Redpath asked, "Is it true that it's often difficult to distinguish who is your friend and who is your enemy? That someone you believe is your friend is actually not, and vice versa? And do your friends sometimes become your enemies and your enemies your friends?" After a moment the students shouted, "True dat!" and, "You know that's no lie!" "Then how," Redpath replied, "can we base our definition of justice on identifying our friends and our enemies if that's so difficult to do?"

There was silence in the room, the silence of thinking, of each student waking to his own thought process. They were grappling with productive resistance. I could see that Dr. Redpath wasn't making the mistake that I'd made of trying to download information to the students or over-perform in an effort to keep their attention. He didn't recite facts or give answers but enlisted each of the students in a collaborative activity as they explored the meaning of the questions. He questioned them relentlessly, asking, Who are you? Where do you come from? How do you know? Their responses triggered trapdoors that led to deeper levels of questioning. A number of students who prided themselves on always having the right answers challenged Redpath until they sensed that their answers were contradictory. One wisely exclaimed, "Yo, Doc, you fuckin' with my head!"

Which was true in a sense. He fucked with their heads in the most loving, compassionate way possible, by pointing to their minds and asking them to think. He held space in the classroom for that to occur without ever being authoritarian or dismissive. This was not a skill I'd acquired; I knew how to perform a teaching show and how to use force, but not how to drop that self-centered effort and shift the focus onto the students.

Although I didn't know it at the time because I hadn't read it, Dr. Redpath was walking them through the first book of Plato's *Republic*. Turning to the photocopied packets that he'd distributed, he assigned speaking roles in the dialogue and we read it aloud. He'd frequently interrupt the reading to ask questions and to probe deeper into the text. I'd never seen the students so immersed in class, and several complained when it ended. If someone had asked me before whether the lesson would work, I would have said that trying to teach Plato would never work. Some of the students were barely literate and wouldn't enjoy struggling with a text that was the bane of so many college freshmen. I was wrong. By demonstrating his faith in philosophical inquiry, Dr. Redpath affirmed the students' capacity to grow in mind. Making the dialogue come alive meant re-creating it in the classroom together.

Observing Dr. Redpath teach was revelatory. All learning is conversational, an intimate exchange between student and teacher that does not necessarily anticipate outcomes. This conversation could take many forms, through speaking or writing or even silence. As many conversations were, it was not always linear, and often its value was not measurable in quantifiable terms. Most important, the conversation was intimate and alive, its parameters and expressions constantly changing in response to its participants.

I thought about how this idea related to my teaching and to my writing as well. I grew up in Scientists' Cliffs, a small community established on the shores of the Chesapeake Bay by paleontologists who discovered an abundance of fossils buried there. The image of digging fossils out of the cliffs was an image for my own creative processes. Existing at the border between water and earth, these fragile remains were excavated by hand. Often they emerged broken, partial, and fragmentary. My writing process was similarly one of accumulation as shards of language swam to the surface. Arranging these elements was an ongoing effort to find my voice and to help others find theirs.

Though I had to keep digging to find my own way in the classroom, a shift had occurred. Dr. Redpath showed me a way of teaching that was relational, based in an ongoing exchange between equals. His willingness to meet the students and to share his mind with them spoke to the failure of prisons that operated through silencing and separation to rehabilitate anyone. There was no healing without intimacy and the vulnerability that it required.

I wondered what motivated Dr. Redpath to come to the island and teach. All of the teachers I had met had experienced some kind of trauma. One day after class we had lunch together in the officers' mess hall. We talked about our childhood memories of school and he told me a story, saying, "You know, when I was growing up in Brooklyn I ran around with a bunch of kids from Mafia families. One day, some older boys from outside the neighborhood started hanging around the schoolyard during lunch and selling drugs. Usually they'd give free samples for a few weeks until they got a kid hooked, then start demanding payment. I never took any, but a lot of my friends did. The father of one of my friends, Vic Baglia, sent word to these teenage hoods that they weren't to do business anywhere near school grounds. They ignored him. A week later, I was walking to school in the morning with my buddies. Spiked on one of the fence posts around the school was the severed head of one of the dealers. Its mouth was open, and its tongue had been pulled out. Only the whites of the eyes showed. I kneeled and threw up on my school shoes. No one saw any of the older boys in the neighborhood again." Dr. Redpath smiled, sipping his soda. I recalled the student who'd told him on his first day, "Yo, Doc, you fuckin' with my head!" and we both laughed so hard we spit our drinks on the table.

The Cove

AFTER MY FIRST month at GRVC, Paige met me at a bar near Queens Plaza for a drink. Since I'd been promoted, I saw her only during staff meetings. She wanted to hear all about my new girlfriend, having heard the gossip from Jay, who no longer spoke to me or returned my calls. Twenty minutes late, she came into the bar shaking, a strange smile on her face. Light rain slicked the pavement outside, carrying the smell of the streets inside as the door swung shut behind her.

She sat on a barstool next to me, brushed herself off, and told me what had happened. Exiting the Q101, she'd stopped inside Dunkin's for a cup of coffee. After waiting in a long line, she reached into her wallet to pay. It was empty. She wondered if she'd lost track of her cash or whether someone had picked her wallet. Pushing the unopened cup back at the cashier, she apologized. The woman wearily glanced at the line snaking behind her and told her to take it. Paige thanked her and promised to bring the money the next day. She started walking the half-block to the F train. A group of three young men walked up, swaggering in their baggy jeans. One of them yelled, "Hey baby, where you goin'? Yo, you got a fat ass for a white girl."

She headed toward him.

"First of all, I'm not your baby. And you can't even see my ass yet."

His friends chimed in.

"Aw, shit, Styles, you gonna let her dis you like that?"

"Yo, bitch, I know you ain't talkin' to me! Don't make me smack the shit outta you!"

He stepped closer. His eyes were bloodshot and he was younger than she'd thought, probably fifteen or sixteen, soon to be on his way to the juvenile unit on Rikers. She loosened the lid on her coffee cup. As he swung his arm back, she threw the scalding coffee in his face. Screaming, he fell to his knees and clawed his face and she ran toward the subway station, her long legs churning. I laughed, picturing her sprinting in high heels on slick pavement. Looking over her shoulder, she saw the other two boys chasing her. Pedestrians parted as she raced by, rounding the corner.

Feeling the boys coming closer, she'd flashed back to the night in her hut in Madagascar where she'd served in the Peace Corps. Moonlight blazed through the front windows and someone shrieked outside. The bodyguard she'd hired for night duty shouted as he crashed through the flimsy door with a spear jutting from his belly. She scrambled to her feet and smashed the screened window of her room as a group of men ran in after the guard. Sounds of shattering glass mingled with angry cries followed her as she fled into the humid darkness. The bodyguard survived, but the thieves were never found.

A police cruiser was parked by the stairwell of the train station, an officer leaning against the passenger door. Paige ran toward him, and his eyes followed her route, watching the two kids behind her exchange glances and quickly stop as though they were lost, then turn around and stroll back up the block. Out of breath, she bent over and placed her hands on her thighs. The officer waited, expecting her to say something. She looked up, gritting her teeth, and smiled.

"What was that all about, Miss?" he asked.

"Nothing, officer. Guys chase me like that all the time."

Paige grinned and raised her eyebrows. I'd missed her. I reminded her about the morning when I'd rescued her coffee from the subway thief, the morning of my first day on the island. This time I hadn't been there to protect her, so she'd had to use her beverage as a weapon. If I ran into a kid in Queens Plaza with burns on his face I'd know him. Reaching over and holding her hand, I interlaced my fingers between hers. I felt like we were runaways who'd escaped some calamity and were free to be together. But we were not; she'd been my brother's girlfriend. They'd broken up long ago, once she'd tired of his emotional distance. My brother and I both sought distance in different ways, I wanted to tell her; we craved it for good reasons.

She asked if she could tell me something that she couldn't share with anyone else. I nodded, squeezing her hand. That afternoon she'd made a big decision. After her classes, she'd read a newspaper article titled "Woman

Mauled by Hellhounds." A snapshot of the victim, a young woman about our age, stared at her in grainy detail. In the headline photo, the victim was smiling at the photographer. How was a grown woman killed by dogs? She'd heard of babies and kids being fatally wounded by vicious pit bulls, but not a grownup with the strength to fend them off.

The dogs that had torn out her throat were being kept by two married lawyers for an Aryan skinhead locked up in Pelican Bay. They'd legally adopted him, and the Aryan wanted to start his own breeding business from prison. The dogs were his first investment. They were raised on his girlfriend's farm, and she told him she couldn't keep them after they turned feral and began killing her neighbor's livestock. Enter his attorneys, who were infatuated with him and sent him letters about their sexual fantasies of being dominated by him. They offered to house the wild dogs in their San Francisco apartment. Other residents in the building complained. They attacked other dogs at the local park and the lawyers took them out less and less. Returning home from work, the victim was on the second day of her period. She was petite, 5'1" and 110 pounds, much smaller than the calves the dogs had gutted a few months before. Her key in her hand, she was startled as a door down the hallway opened.

It didn't make sense. Paige had cried on a couch in the faculty lounge, hiding her face behind the unfolded paper. There wasn't any protection in a society shaped by events that were increasingly unnatural. Why should she fight to change it, to be a peacemaker in the midst of this violence? Grinding against the correctional system, she found her heart and mind depleted as the cycle repeated daily: detainees shipped to the island on buses, filling the jails as others were released to the city, soon to return. She had always said to herself that once she no longer enjoyed her work at Horizon, she'd leave. She didn't want to become institutionalized like some of the counselors we knew who'd worked on the island so long they seemed perpetually beat down, drained of some essential hue. She hoped Gloria would understand.

I did and had actually promised myself the same thing, though I wasn't sure if I'd have the courage to follow through. Was it also time for me to quit, to leave on the Q101 and not return? Could I run away with Paige, get a private berth on a train to New Orleans, fuck her senseless as we whispered convicts' slang in each other's ears? What would my brother say if he found out? What would Lauren do?

I was quickly becoming drunk. I finished my whiskey and stared at the bestiary of sports pennants hanging behind the bar: Bulls, Bears, and Blackhawks nailed to the wall like enemy scalps or gang flags. Two TVs were mounted to the ceiling at either end. Patrons stared at them through smoke clouds, chained to their stools by cigarettes binding their hands to the nearest ashtray. Their faces appeared partially melted, streaked with red and yellow drips.

I turned to Paige and said, "Hey, see those people at the end of the bar? What's wrong with their faces? Am I fucked up already or are they melting?"

"You're seeing things. Relax. You don't have to look at them. Leave them alone."

"I'm not. They're staring at us. We're the Vikings storming their hamlet."

"So why don't you go over and talk to them and make a peace offering."

"I ran out of peace offerings once I saw your beautiful face walk through the door."

"Yeah, right. Tell the truth: You never had any."

"You inspire me to be a better person."

"Really? Because you're being very bad right now."

"Am I? Is noticing your beauty so terrible? Maybe if my brother had more often you wouldn't have left him."

"Hold on. There were many reasons for that. And it's none of your business."

"If you say so, beautiful."

"The same words over and over. Can't you say something original?"

We sat and watched the game. Dennis Rodman's hair glowed with leopard spots as he streaked under the basket and snagged an offensive rebound. He threw an outlet pass to Jordan waiting at half court to scoop the ball up and weave toward the basket, freezing defenders in place with his crossover dribble. At the top of the key he faked the pass, then went baseline, accelerating as Gary Payton slid in front of him and braced for contact that never arrived because Jordan had leapt over him, hanging horizontally in the air above the rim before he slammed the basket. Shouts in the bar echoed the roaring crowd on the television.

I said, "Did you see that?"

Paige said, "Jordan's the best, right? That's why kids shoot each other for his sneakers."

"No, those punks just do it for street cred. Listen to these barstool jocks carry on. Assholes."

"You don't see Lake or Captain Ortega in here, do you? So why are you worried? No one here knows us. No one's going to bother you."

"Why would we run into them?"

"The Cove is a CO hangout. That's what Latasha said when I told her that I was coming here to meet you."

"Oh, shit. That explains it. You and Officer Price are tight like that now? Latasha?"

"Of course. Just because you aren't friendly doesn't mean I'm not. Listen, everything is fine now. We're just watching the game along with everyone else. You've listened to my stories, and I want to hear yours."

"Actually, I also have something to tell you. First, let me get us another round."

The bartender was chatting with a group of guys at the other end of the bar. I slid off my stool and started to walk over to her.

I said, "Excuse me, Miss, can I trouble you for a minute?" She turned her head slowly and gave me the stink eye. One of the men she'd been talking to licked foam off his thin moustache and pulled down the brim of his NYPD baseball cap.

"What you drinkin', pardner?" he slurred.

I ignored him. "Two shots of Jack, please." He continued to stare.

"Hey, pal, you don't have to ignore me. I was just bein' friendly. Where you from anyway?" He glanced at his buddies and nodded.

"I just came from Rikers Island. You know where that is, right?"

"Sure do." The guy stared into his beer glass as the bartender reluctantly slid the shots in front of me. I wanted these tanked CO's to mistake me for an inmate, for the dream that had sprung from their skulls to beat them half to death. I wanted to be an outlaw, to seduce Paige and run away with her as fugitives. Mostly I wanted to be expelled from the island, removed and barred entrance, fired by the Board of Education and dumped by Lauren. I wanted to burn the whole fucking prison of my life to the ground.

A bearded man two seats away chimed in. "Ever thought about cutting your hair? I hear they make you do that on Rikers."

"That's right," said the first man, raising his eyes from his glass and grinning. "They cut it for you, shave it close as a lamb's ass, don't they, boy?"

I reached over and removed the man's NYPD cap, placing it on the second man's head backward.

"Much better. Now I can really understand you two. That hideous cap was getting in the way. Trust me, both of you look much better now. Keep your mouths shut and we'll get along."

Paige had walked over to me and she grabbed my arm, pulling me away. "C'mon, forget about them. Let's enjoy our drinks."

We went back to our seats and raised our shots.

I said, "To new beginnings." Our glasses clinked. If we'd been listening, we'd have noticed how quiet the bar had become, the only noise distant cheers on the televisions. One of the men came over behind us and tapped Paige on her shoulder.

"Hey, woman, your boyfriend needs to learn some manners. Didn't they teach him that in lockup?"

She stood up, a head taller than he in her heels. He was every guard who'd ever pissed her off, who'd talked to other men in the room as though she weren't there, dismissing anything she could say before she spoke. He was the boy who'd harassed and chased her, the Nazi who'd bred killer dogs.

"My name isn't woman, shithead. Who are you anyway? Let me guess, you just got off work after beating inmates at C-74 all day and now you're out jacking off with your buddies. Well, we work there too, so fuck off, asshole!"

The man lurched back, confused. He pointed at me.

"He said he was from the island, so me and my buddies figured he was some 'vic who'd just been released and was trying to break our balls."

I smiled.

"No, I'm just a lowly prison teacher. Trying to rehabilitate lost souls, just like you guys. Care, custody, and control, right? You're a fucking joke. If you have a problem with me, why don't we step outside?"

He raised his hands as though I had a gun pointed at him.

"Fuck you," I yelled, then walked outside and stood in the green and violet sheen of bar lights, waiting for them. I prayed they'd stagger out of the bar, pacing furiously and pounding my fist into the palm of my hand. I couldn't see Paige anymore, though I knew she was close by, heard her pleading with me to calm down.

"Relax, they aren't coming," she said. Another disappointment. We stood alone in the street, then eventually walked together to the subway. Christ, I thought, mistaken for an inmate. It was almost funny.

Pink Leaves

ON RIKERS THERE were multiple literacies, various grids laid over the prisoners' words and their worlds. Hybrid languages continually evolved, gaining textures and losing others. Words merged, were squeezed and coaxed from the mouth like paint spread across canvas: the cerulean blue of *Dios Mios* brushing against the brick red of *Damu* and the soft pink of *Baby Momma*. Most conversations were nonverbal, a click of the tongue, a rubbing of palms or a steady gaze that may have found its target or gone beyond it.

I knew something was wrong when a student named Barrett Price gave me that stare after I asked him to read aloud in class. Not an angry or aggressive sneer, but a look that was a wall, a refusal so deep it didn't need the word "No." Barrett never said much and he had the biggest fists I'd ever seen, fists the size of Sonny Liston's, bone crushers attached to his muscled forearms. His appearance and demeanor, the language he was speaking, so to speak, was intended to keep others at a distance. Which it did. Barrett wasn't Blood or Crip, Jamaican Posse or Latin King; he was unaffiliated with any gang as only the toughest or most foolhardy inmates were. And he'd paid for it: I'd heard him describe being jumped by a group of Latin Kings one night while he was asleep. Once he woke up he beat them with those massive hands, staggering from bed and ripping a phone from a nearby wall to bludgeon his assailants. That's how Barrett preferred to use a phone, not as a communication device but as a sledgehammer.

Every day I asked Barrett if he wanted to read, and every day he stared at me with the same expression. I figured it was just respectful for me to keep asking, in case he ever changed his mind. One day after the other students had lined up to go to lunch, he asked to talk to me privately. In a low voice, his eyes staring at the floor, he told me he wanted to read in class but couldn't because he was severely dyslexic and often couldn't understand the words. He asked if I would work with him one-on-one to improve his reading. I agreed and we set up a time the following day after class. Even though I'd never taught remedial reading, I was so excited that Barrett had spoken to me that I decided to teach myself how. We began going over easy class readings together during the lunch break, including passages from Richard Wright's *Black Boy* and Steinbeck's *Of Mice and Men*. Whenever Barrett encountered an unfamiliar word, he wrote it in his journal so he could slowly build a vocabulary list that we could study together.

A couple of weeks later, I asked him to bring something he liked to read since he'd told me he was allowed to have magazines in his cell. The next day he carefully handed me a tattered copy of *I ♥ My American Pit-bull Terrier* as though it were the coda to some sacred text. Barrett said I could hold onto it until our following tutoring session, and I thought that whatever happened, I had better not lose that magazine. The ads from breeders were the best, with captions like *Bam-Bam and Red Chief pups—get one now!* and *Black Mamba's sire is fifty percent panther, sure to produce an outstanding litter!*

Doggie porn, with centerfolds of massive pit bulls showing off barrel chests, anvil-sized heads filled with rows of sharks' teeth. In the background of the photos, trailer park yards enclosed inside wire mesh fences. Other prisons, places of torture where dogs were fed gunpowder that destroyed the lining of their stomachs and were taught to swing from tires suspended on ropes. Thankfully for our purpose, the articles were written in barely legible third-grade prose that Barrett could read. Most of the text was promotional material about the dogs, their bloodlines, and how they were raised. I understood why Barrett loved this magazine and these dogs so much: He identified with their strength and fearlessness. They were his heroes.

When I told Lauren about teaching Barrett, she talked about one of the autistic kids she worked with, a brilliant three-year-old named Richard who'd been diagnosed with mild autism. Twice a week, she traveled to the Upper West Side apartment where Richard and his parents lived to do play therapy with him. One day, he inexplicably began crying and would not stop. When she asked him why he was crying, he pointed to a window in his room and said, "The leaves are green, but I want them to be pink." She smiled and said, "I understand how you feel. Sometimes we want the leaves to be pink, but they're not. We just have to accept that they are green. And later, they will change color. We can enjoy them now that they are green and know that someday when they are pink we will also enjoy them."

I guess Richard found this teaching less than persuasive, since he continued to bawl for several minutes, repeating, "But I want them to be pink." Still, his rage and dismay did not change what was. Inevitably both the lush beauty of green leaves and the hot flush of pink blossoms resisted human will as surely as meteors fell from the sky and skies darkened during storms. Like him, I was slowly learning to accept the limits of what I could change, trying to believe that helping one prisoner at a time was enough.

Strong and White

IN PRISON, ONE makes fast and deep bonds that could rival those of any hostages and captors, friendships shaped by continual danger and dependency. I'd first met Donovan, a math and science teacher, when I'd been transferred to GRVC. He'd grown up in Brooklyn, where he had taught in city high schools for several years. Donovan was a charismatic teacher to whom the inmates responded, giving him their respect and attention. The same students who would disrupt my class and challenge me day after day would go to his class right afterward and listen to him describe the rules of algebra. I'd peek into his classroom and they would be diligently working on whatever math problems he'd written on the board, the only sound that of graphite scratching paper. I was envious of his success, unsure of what I was doing wrong. When I told him I was frustrated because the same guys who were acting up in my class seemed fine in his, he graciously said he'd speak to them. He didn't lecture me or give me advice, but just offered to help. I was embarrassed by my anger and impatience, ashamed to reveal the parts of myself that I didn't like.

As the school population at GRVC grew, I befriended the two school officers Strong and White. Officer Strong was of course a burly man with a soft voice who invited me to lift weights with him in the officers' weight room during our lunch breaks. I joined him a couple of times a week, and in the weight room his voice would suddenly raise as he shouted out the reps and attacked the weights, dropping them to the floor with shuddering thuds.

Officer White commanded the desk where inmates checked in as they entered the school area. Calm but forceful, she commanded the students' respect through her easygoing but firm approach. Sitting at her desk checking ID cards, she'd really be looking at each of the men with recognition as they passed by her to line up against the concrete wall where Strong frisked them. White and Strong didn't treat them like animals but like young men who could have been their kinfolk or the children of their neighborhood friends, which some of them most likely were. And when one of the students called me a white devil in front of the class and I asked him to step outside into the corridor to talk, Strong and White did not intervene. They watched us and let me handle it, understanding that the prisoners were students in that space and that I needed to earn their respect.

Students were allowed to leave the class one at a time once they were given the bathroom pass, a laminated sheet the size of a large postcard. One afternoon I heard scuffling in the hallway, and as I ran to the door I saw Lazy Eye and Menace trading blows. Stepping forward, I grabbed Lazy Eye and saw Donovan on the other side wrap his arms around Menace. Surprisingly, both of them actually stopped fighting and we were able to separate them before White and Strong came running. Menace had a bloody nose, but otherwise the damage appeared negligible. They continued to glare at each other, though, which I knew meant that nothing had been settled. Lazy Eye was a leader of the Latin Kings, and Menace was a captain in the Bloods. Both of their gangs attended Horizon, and almost all of our students belonged to one of the gangs or the other. Barrett Price was one of the few students so fearsome he didn't need to be in a gang for protection, but he was an exception.

Now that Lazy Eye and Menace had squared off, the danger for a gang war in the school area was high. Inmates had always respected the school as a conflict-free zone and I'd never seen a fight there before. Everything had changed. The school had become another battleground, another contested area of the prison. We had been engulfed by the island, overrun by its inhabitants' relentless violence and their struggle to survive. I called Gloria to report the incident and braced myself for what would happen.

The following afternoon, a flood of new students arrived at the door of the school area. At least fifteen guys I'd never seen before, and I knew all of the regulars. An ominous energy rippled along that line of new arrivals as they quietly scanned the area, a massive cobra coiled to strike. Blood foot soldiers, they were looking for one man. With only two officers on duty, it would be difficult to stop them once they saw their chance to retaliate.

Officer White didn't flinch; she placed the men against the wall, called me over to the check-in line, and asked, "Do you recognize any of these guys?" When I said no, she actually stood up at her desk, a sign she was going to lay down some law.

"All of you, I know what you're here for. Not today. Forget about it. Now turn around and start walking out the door. You're all going back to your cells."

Silence as the line slowly turned and slithered back out. I was surprised and outraged by their boldness. Did they really think that would work? That we would just let them waltz into the school and attack one another, destroy what we had worked so hard to build? They didn't care about any of us civilian workers or guards; they'd just regroup and try to find an opportunity somewhere else. The gangs were many-headed Hydras that regenerated when their heads were cut off. They had no sense of honor or fair play, and they didn't fight one-on-one. Asleep, in the shower, at chow, anyone could be jumped at any time.

I'd learned two things after this encounter. One, I responded in emergency situations and took action without hesitating. My instinct was fight, not flight. Two, I could trust Donovan to do the same. I had his back and he had mine. We grew closer after that incident, having to rely on each other for our lives. We had been in danger. One of those men could have had a weapon. The other inmates in class could have rushed into the corridor and joined the fight. In those moments of chaos, nothing was certain. Razors could be suddenly spit from beneath tongues, shanks pulled from pants legs. In a place where lawlessness became its own containment, what was the meaning of limits? When I wrapped my arms around Lazy Eye and pushed him against a wall, I entered the unknown beyond the boundaries of my civilian role. I'd forfeited its protections, released the thread that led through the labyrinth.

Yard Blues

VIOLENT INCIDENTS NEVER occurred singularly. They happened in bursts, through some unseen synergy. Turned away at the gates of Horizon, the Bloods waited, slumbering in the coils of vengeful dreams. I was called into a meeting with Frank Coppola, the deputy warden of GRVC. He announced that the rapper Rah Digga had volunteered to perform a free concert in the yard for the inmates, and Coppola wanted to invite the Horizon students. The guys would be excited. Many of them fancied themselves amateur rappers and I'd heard them freestyle in their circle ciphers, challenging each other to spit the best lines.

The story of criminal–turned–famous rapper was a popular narrative, a reinvention of the Horatio Alger myth that entranced poor city kids raised in poverty. It rarely ever happened, and for every Biggie or Nas there were hundreds who emulated the lifestyle, deceiving themselves that they could turn suffering into affluence. A few of the inmates had genuine skills. I heard them rapping before class began, though nothing they said was original, every lyric shaded with desperation, calling for some compensatory power or dominance they lacked. Their rhymes re-inscribed the walls of their prison, fencing them inside what kept them powerless.

On the morning of the Rikers concert, Rah Digga's sound crew set up in the recreation yard, an asphalt square divided into four basketball courts. While we waited for her to appear, more houses of inmates were escorted into the yard until there were more than one hundred inmates crowded there. I played a pickup game with some older inmates, which many other teachers wouldn't do because they socialized only with the inmates who went to Horizon. I understood that, because without uniforms or radios we civilians didn't have much authority outside of the school walls.

After the fight between Lazy Eye and Menace, I strangely felt closer to the inmates. I wasn't afraid of shooting hoops with prisoners I didn't know, and running on the court with them, slapping high fives and laughing, it was easy to momentarily forget where I was. Then someone shouted my name. Deputy Coppola wanted to speak to me. I left the game and found him near one of the entry gates. He said that my shirt wasn't appropriate to wear in the yard, since it looked gang-related. I looked down at the blue t-shirt I was wearing decorated with a design of a crown. "What gang?" I asked. "Just take it off," he answered, "or leave the yard." Turning my back to him, I peeled the sweaty shirt off, turned it inside out, and stretched the damp cloth over my chest and back, the panther and snake tattooed on my arm. "This suit you?" I asked. He nodded, and I returned to the game.

Finally, after at least an hour, Rah Digga appeared. She'd been told by the D.O.C. not to wear any makeup or anything provocative. Dressed in a camouflage jumpsuit, boots, and a baseball cap, she'd followed instructions. Her sound system consisted of two speakers, a mic, and a couple of bongos that were being played by Lazy Eye and one of his friends. I wondered how she was going to keep the restless crowd's attention. Then she started rapping, and the rhythm of her words, the spaces between them, drifted in sinuous vapor trails through the audience, mesmerizing us as though we were snakes in baskets. I turned around to glimpse a sea of bobbing heads, Donovan grooving next to me. Her lyrics spoke of life, of its endurance and vitality even in the darkest cages, and as it lifted us she responded, bringing the flame of her voice into the circle of light. The shoddy speakers, the stumbling bongos, none of it mattered when the voice emerged, calling the people back home.

Suddenly, a shout erupted. I turned as Lazy Eye and his friend dropped the bongo drums and started running. Three Bloods I recognized from class reached into the legs of their sweats and pulled out ten-inch shanks, then began chasing Lazy Eye around the periphery of the yard. A sheet of tension rippled over the crowd, and the prison alarm whooped at ear-shattering volume. Guards must have whisked Rah Digga away, given that she disappeared. I hoped she didn't feel like I had during the weed incident at West Facility, like she'd given her heart and soul and the inmates had shit on it.

I saw what was happening: The Bloods were chasing Lazy Eye, running him down as they circled back toward me.

I froze, watching riot guards rush into the yard. Turtles, the inmates called them, wearing helmets, gloves, and shank-proof vests as they wielded heavy batons. As Lazy Eye rounded a corner, the deputy warden clocked him in the jaw with his radio and he crumpled to the pavement, shaking on the ground. Other guards swung their heavy batons, striking the Bloods who had shanks and slamming them to the ground. All the other inmates immediately fell as though shot and sprawled face down on the asphalt as the guards swarmed among them, clubbing anyone who resisted. I stood there, not moving. Time dilated, sirens whooping across the pavement, the ridges in the guards' vests visible as ripples in a tremendous black wave sweeping closer.

One of them stood in front of me, cursing as though I were the one he'd been sent to subdue. I saw his lips moving behind the Plexiglas shield of his helmet, droplets of spit on the inside of the visor. He raised his baton, his other gloved hand clenched into a fist. I glanced at the periphery of the yard and saw that all of my co-workers had fled. I was alone, my only identification an ID card that hung from a lanyard around my neck. The guard spotted it and yelled, "What the fuck are you doing here, civilian? Leave!" His voice rang out across the silence of the yard, freezing the tableau of a hundred men lying face down, fingers interlaced behind their heads while the turtles loomed above them. Something inside me shifted, breaking my paralysis. Nodding at the guard, I turned and rushed toward a break in the fence.

Lost Dalí

ONE MORNING, NOT long after the riot in the yard, I arrived at Rikers still wearing my blue flower print shirt from the night before, having begged for train fare outside Grand Central Terminal. Teeth grinding, my long hair tangled and filthy, I was buzzing on coke given to me by a man who'd claimed he was Salvador Dalí's cousin.

How had this happened? My double life had been fraying for months; I was spending more nights in my studio, telling Lauren I was too exhausted to travel to her place in Midtown. After a couple hours of sleep, I'd leave the apartment and prowl the bars of Lower Manhattan, making sure to call Lauren from a grungy bathroom and tell her goodnight. A favorite spot for these calls was Manitoba's, a punk rock bar on the Lower East Side run by Richard "Handsome Dick" Manitoba, the singer of the legendary band The Dictators. It was there one night that I saw Nick Tosches' beautiful red-headed girlfriend fall halfway down a flight of stairs in her stilettos and climb back up unscathed except for one broken heel dangling behind her. I wanted whatever she was on, though that night I was drinking Jack on the rocks. With each sip, the tension in my skull relaxed. I started talking to a pretty blonde with sculpted calves, sliding onto the stool next to her. Someone punched the Ramones on the jukebox and I asked her to dance. She laughed and shook her head.

Suddenly, a stocky man with slicked-back hair appeared behind her. She introduced him as her friend Rocco. He smiled at me and called over another woman, named Michelle. Soon the four of us were buying rounds of shots and clinking glasses, the girls singing the choruses together. *Ba ba ba bamp ba ba ba ba bamp, I wanna be sedated.*

Rocco said he worked in construction. He was proud of once having hurled a full beer bottle at former Mayor David Dinkins. He claimed to have hit the mayor and though I doubted him, Rocco's charm made these outrageous boasts seem harmless. After I bought him a couple of rounds he confessed he'd come over when he spotted me hitting on his girl, but that when I stood up to shake his hand he'd realized I was too big to fuck with. Michelle was fascinated by my tales of prison escapades, so when Rocco suggested we all take a cab to the West Side I agreed, calculating that I could stay out for two more hours before crashing to get up for work the next day.

In the cab Rocco yelled at the driver, telling him which radio station to play and which route to take as I nestled between the girls in the back seat. We drove on 14th Street back toward my studio, then past the Hellfire Club to Ninth Avenue. This was before that area became gentrified, when the Meatpacking District still represented its name. We clambered into the Red Room, one of my favorite West Side haunts decorated in bordello velvet and plush red Victorian couches. I bought Michelle a drink and eased next to her on one of the couches, diamonds of light from the chandelier above swimming across her bare shoulders. I reached my arm around her and pulled her closer.

"Hey B!" Rocco shouted. "Come here just a sec, let me talk to ya," he said, and when he saw my face, "It's very important, I promise. Michelle, he'll be right back, I promise, okay sweetheart?"

She shrugged as I pulled away, her sequined dress shimmering.

"Hey B," he said, leaning close to me, "I need to ask you for a favor. See, I'm doing business with some wise guys across the street at that joint Bretanno's. All I need for you to do is to walk in with me and stand there. They'll see you got my back. You're a good friend."

"I don't know, I was really having a good time with Michelle."

"I know, I know, stud. I can tell that she's quite smitten with you too. You're a gentle giant, right? But the guys I need to talk to don't know that, they'll just see how damn big you are. And that you're with me, as a friend. That puts my mind at ease too. I need you, B."

The duck game flashed through my mind, but I was too drunk to care. And I wanted to return to Michelle, to have her to myself undisturbed. I didn't believe Rocco's bullshit about the Mob and I'd been to Bretanno's, a popular lounge on Ninth. After lighting two cigars and handing one to me, Rocco marched across the street, motioning for me to follow him. Doing business? Wise guys? I'd seen all the movies; the only wise guys left were doing life in super-max facilities. The Mob was dead, and even if it wasn't, why would it entertain a beer-bottle-throwing punk like Rocco? I thought why not call his bluff.

"Let's go," I urged, "I got your back, Rocco. They won't touch you."

"Yes, brother! Just stand next to me, and we'll be in and out."

It was past 1 A.M. when we stumbled through the door. Usually at that hour on a Thursday night Bretanno's was dead, but this night the bar was packed, and after scanning the room Rocco nodded his head and strolled toward a table in back. Seated there, a group of old guys dressed in suits turned their heads as he approached, looking at him through binocular-sized glasses. The gears in my brain locked. No way, you've got to be shitting me, I thought. I'd drunk in Bretanno's many times, and had never seen elderly patrons there, much less ones wearing dark suits and sporting glasses the size of safety goggles.

Rocco turned and pointed at me, and the gangsters swiveled in my direction. I froze as though my legs were already encased in cement, dragging the bottom of the East River. Rocco told me to wait for him at the bar where I watched him talk to the old men, waving his arms like a used-car salesman selling a getaway car.

Ten minutes later he sauntered over to me, smiling. I asked him how it went and he said, "Fine. No problem. They just wanted to talk." My instincts had been honed on Rikers, and I knew that the situation he'd dragged me into had been dangerous. He offered to buy me a drink since I had guts and was a good friend. My self-imposed curfew was shot. I'd passed the stage of drunkenness when fatigue registers and had entered a kind of floating yet lucid sensation that more booze cannot diminish. I didn't know what was real and what was a waking dream.

As Rocco left to call the women over, a short man with long dark hair and a midnight-blue cravat appeared next to me. He raised his glass.

"Let us drink to art, and to the beautiful ladies of Manhattan," he drawled in a thick Spanish accent. "Are you an artist, my friend?" he asked.

I said I was a writer, and he grabbed onto my elbow.

"I knew you were an artist, my friend. Do you know who I am? I am the cousin of Salvador Dalí!" I smirked. First the Mob, now Dalí's cousin?

He stared at me and said, "I see you do not believe me, young man, but I will prove it to you. My cousin Salvador gave me several of his original . paintings. I paint as well. I will show you; we shall go to my apartment! Do you do coke?"

Since I'd just survived being whacked, I wasn't in a position to refuse free drugs. When Rocco and the girls arrived, Dalí's cousin repeated his exuberant claims. Once he mentioned coke, they quickly accepted his invitation and we jumped in a cab to his Upper West Side loft. I told myself I had to accompany them, had to see if these supposed Dalí paintings were real, had to discover the truth. It was a quest to find the hidden masterpieces of twentieth-century surrealism. This was a mission worth sacrifice, I told myself as Michelle held my hand, her long index finger rubbing against my palm.

As we rode the elevator to the fifteenth floor, I inspected Cousin Dalí's blue cravat. Maybe he worked for the old mobsters smoking cigars and their hit men were waiting for us inside. Or perhaps a seismic shift in the landscape of twentieth-century surrealist art was about to occur, the discovery of a stash of authentic paintings kept hidden by a reclusive eccentric whose hunger for adoring company had finally compelled him to divulge his secret. I didn't imagine he was seducing me (insert Man Ray photo of a black stiletto held under a woman's chin, her long tongue extending serpent-like to touch the straps).

Our reflections were distorted in the oval mirror Dalí's cousin laid before us, its silvering flaking away as though eaten by disease, the promised lines carving our swollen faces. Paintings hung on the apartment walls, a kaleidoscope of greens and browns, occasionally a swath of red flaring on the canvas. Murky and poorly composed, they no more resembled original masterworks than two men dressed up in a horse costume resemble a horse. I thought of Goya's black paintings, garish and horrific murals rendered on the plaster walls of his house. An image of Saturn as a leering cannibal, eyes bulging as he grasped the decapitated body of his son, preparing to take another bite.

What was I looking for, an electrified swordfish swathed in lion's fur? Or the actual Dalí painting the artist donated to Rikers Island in 1965 when he became ill and canceled his scheduled visit with the inmates, a hastily made sketch of the crucifixion that was stolen by guards thirty-eight years later and never recovered? Although three officers confessed to taking part in the heist and a fourth was implicated but never convicted, the lost Dalí remains missing. Painted with India ink, the original can now be seen online only, most distinct the jagged thorns crowning Christ's bowed head. Where was the lost Rikers Dalí? Would it ever be found?

How could I become angry with anyone except myself for momentarily entertaining the absurd? Rocco's girl reached over, stroked my thigh, and said, "Mmmm, you have strong legs. You play soccer or somethin'?"

The sensation of her hand across the denim of my jeans was exquisite, every hair follicle sensitized, a field of vibration extending two inches from the surface of my skin. I found Michelle in another room, ran my fingers along the smooth skin on the inside of her forearm. Whenever it seemed we were about to kiss, Dali's cousin appeared, insisting we look at another page from his portfolio of child-like sketches. I blinked, and dawn's gray light suddenly brushed the tall windows of the apartment, a pigeon cooing on the window ledge. As the girls gently swatted his small hands away from their hips, Dali's cousin told us we must leave, ushering us along a cramped hallway and back into the elevator.

We staggered onto Seventh Avenue and 56th Street, exiting into the waking city. Once the others were gone, I suddenly remembered, I had to go to Rikers. Reaching into my wallet, I confirmed there was nothing left, not a dime. No money on my MetroCard. I didn't use ATMs and didn't have an ATM card or a credit card.

I started panhandling outside the subway station for change, averting my eyes as I asked strangers for subway fare, forcing myself to speak more loudly. I tried to mask my humiliation by smiling, as though the absurdity of my predicament was most surprising to me. It was true that I'd never begged for money before, that I had only asked for a few dollars from friends and later paid them back, and that I was often callous to the filthy people huddled in mounds in the station vestibules who bleated out pleas for assistance. Once Lauren had said to me that at least I could look at them and smile, acknowledge that they're human. But I did not, and now I was the one asking for a handout.

Waves of morning commuters accustomed to beggars did not even look as they passed by. Wearing my long-sleeved shirt printed with tiny blue flowers and my baggy jeans, I was a clown, not threadbare enough to garner sympathy nor assertive enough to convincingly sell the joke. My situation was fully self-inflicted: I had a job, an apartment, and a life, and still I was choosing to drown.

For twenty minutes I wandered up and down the street, watching faces become shuttered when they heard my request, shocked by the tall white man holding out his hand, until eventually a young man frowned and gingerly handed me two bucks as though fearing to touch me. I handed the money to the cashier, and she threw a MetroCard back into the slot without meeting my eyes. I was on my way, the memory of Dali's lost masterpieces fading into a haze behind me.

Hoops

IF THE ISLAND offered a tenuous foothold on my spinning world, it too was in motion. After the riot in the yard, the deputy warden locked down GRVC. I didn't see inmates in the corridors anymore unless they were Horizon students being escorted to or from classes. The guard who'd cursed at me during the melee found me one day in the school area and apologized, which was kind since I'd never have recognized him without his full riot gear.

Because all the inmates involved in the riot had been Horizon students, Strong and White were particularly under pressure to monitor the school. One respite from that daily routine was our weekly basketball game on Wednesday afternoon when Donovan and I took well-behaved students to the indoor gym and played ball with them. The guys looked forward to those games all week, and so did we. Chasing after loose balls, running with them up and down the court, slapping high fives after sweet plays, we bonded in a deeper way. In that space, we were equals. I brought my boom box over from the classroom and rap music echoed off the gymnasium walls. Listening to Method Man & Redman's *Blackout!* album, we could have been on any street court in any borough on a summer afternoon, throwing down dunks for a cheering crowd.

This refuge couldn't last, however. Everything beautiful and good on Rikers was sabotaged eventually. The system recoiled from any semblance of the outside world brought inside its walls and punished those who attempted to challenge its boundaries. On those Wednesday afternoons, passing the ball to my teammates, running down court and crashing the boards until my shirt was drenched, I almost forgot I was on an island whose perpetual state was lockdown.

The dispute that ended Wednesday hoops seemed trivial until it was amplified by a system that needed to exert tremendous energy to keep human beings captive. At one of our monthly meetings, Deputy Warden Coppola announced that an organization that mentored young men in the city was going to send representatives to Horizon on the following Wednesday. We had no objections; they could visit our students at 2 P.M., after the day's classes and our weekly basketball game. Coppola agreed, and the visit was set. It was important that Donovan and I stayed when these representatives came, because our students listened to us.

The next Wednesday, Officer White insisted that we cancel our basketball game and stay in the school area, even though I reminded her that the visitors weren't scheduled to arrive until 2 P.M. We remained in school as 2, 2:15, and 2:30 passed, and still no visitors. There were dozens of reasons why civilians were delayed on the island: alarms, metal detectors, improper identification documents, crossed signals between guards. The students became restless, and several demanded to be taken back to their cells. I asked White if we could take them to the gym and shoot hoops until the guests arrived. She said no; they were on their way and we had to stay put.

By 3 P.M., I was furious. Not only had White dismissed our basketball privileges, now she expected us to wait for an indeterminate time for visitors who may or may not actually show. I cannot overemphasize the intensity of emotion that surrounded the schedule in that environment. The schedule was life, while chaos and entropy were death. The school program was being insulted and devalued, and we were expected to cater to the deputy warden's pet project. The Horizon staff was scheduled to leave, and I soon told White and Strong that we were leaving. If they wanted to keep thirty inmates locked down in the school area until these mentors appeared, they could do that. I strongly recommended that they take our students back to their cells. White and Strong refused, insisting that we stay. I returned to the classroom and explained the situation to the students, including my conversation with the officers. Then I walked out along with my colleagues. The D.O.C. could clean up the mess they'd created without asking me to trade on my good faith with the inmates.

It was not my idea to ask my students to return to their cell blocks. They suggested it, and suddenly I realized that I didn't have to comply with the guards' orders to wait. In that moment, through their simple yet profound defiance, my students taught me that I could make a different choice. Though I'd taught them how to read literature and to write about their experiences, they were teaching me how to resist the narrative I'd internalized about obeying authority. I did not, however, have to face the same consequences as they did for this resistance. Every afternoon I left the island while they remained, attempting to survive until the next school day.

Apparently Officers Strong and White did not appreciate my setting a boundary. The next day, Gloria said that they had filed a formal complaint against me, accusing me of inciting a riot in the school area: After the Horizon staff left, the inmates had again demanded to be taken back to their cells, becoming increasingly hostile as the minutes ticked by. There was no actual riot; no one was assaulted, and eventually the officers did return the inmates to their cell blocks. The supposed mentors never arrived.

At first I laughed off these charges, laughed at the stupidity of Strong and White, laughed at another one of Coppola's embarrassments, first Rah Digga and now these no-shows, laughed at the sudden cancellation of Wednesday hoops, laughed at the students who were so angry they threatened to boycott Horizon, laughed at Gloria hunched over her desk, her right shoulder hiked up to her ear as she pointed her index finger at me. Then I stopped laughing. True, I could respond to these charges and they probably wouldn't hold up, wouldn't result in any official sanction. But I was in the D.O.C.'s house. Their house, their rules. Now that I was seen as a threat they would eliminate me, first by trying official channels, then by other means.

There were stories. Legal-aid workers suddenly flagged over at security checkpoints; vials of cocaine discovered in their briefcases. Drug counselors similarly apprehended when knives appeared in the bags they scanned through metal detectors. All of them set up by Corrections, targeted for elimination from the island. Arguments and appeals didn't matter; once the secreted objects provided tangible evidence of a crime there was no escape from banishment. Now I'd become a target, someone whose expulsion could salve Strong and White's shame and re-establish their authority.

I began checking and double-checking my briefcase and all of my pockets whenever I entered or exited GRVC, even though I knew that wouldn't save me because I'd experienced how easily a trained criminal could pick my pocket at will. Then I stopped bringing the briefcase, leaving everything I needed for the next day in the school area. Strong and White stopped talking to me, and the students stopped coming to class. I was sad, because we'd always been friendly, had talked to one another before the school runs and shot hoops during the weekly basketball games. They felt that I'd betrayed them, and everything changed.

Our students complained that Strong picked them up more infrequently, taking advantage of any reason to delay or to cancel the school run. I had to remember that while I could leave the island at the end of the day, my students could not. My relations with the guards affected them, and I was responsible. Although I tried always to be mindful of where I was and of who had the power to sustain Horizon or to shut it down, I sometimes naturally forgot, became comfortable in the daily routine that I assumed would continue unperturbed. When crises arrived, I was reminded that Horizon was a fragile ecosystem dependent upon the participation of all of us who were essentially locked up together. Once I was labeled a troublemaker, I became a liability for the school and was eligible for Horizon's version of the witness protection plan: a transfer.

The prison education system had been laid bare as another means of controlling the inmates. Educators were welcome inside as long as they focused on improving the prisoners' moral character, making them more compliant, easier to manage. Once the lessons shifted to questioning the system itself and the inequities that undergirded the island's systems of power, systems that originated in the foundations of this country and the violence it perpetuated, we were no longer encouraged to teach. Most of those incarcerated on Rikers had not even been sentenced yet, and still they were treated as the condemned, the guilty, who bore a debt other than being poor and people of color.

After a couple of weeks of paranoia and increasing tension, I received a call from Gloria. She said, simply, return to GMDC. Relinquish your position as school coordinator and return full time to the classroom. I understood that I'd been demoted and also rescued from a possibly harsher fate. Since I'd trained myself to travel light, no briefcase or bags to carry, I left the jail immediately without saying goodbye to Strong or White, riding the bus past Devil Mountain back to the same building where I'd entered Rikers almost three years earlier.

The prison education system on Rikers was broken and corrosive. The adversarial stance of the D.O.C. toward Horizon made every task effortful, and eventually the daily obstacles and relentless hostility exhausted even the most dedicated teachers. A change was needed, a complete transformation of the relationship between guards and teachers from hostile dependents to invested participants. If we could have also offered education to the guards, could have enlisted their participation in our classes in an ongoing dialogue, then we could have become their students as well, better understanding how we could work together to positively influence Rikers. Instead of standing on either side of an uneasy truce between government agencies, between the guards who were suspicious of our intentions and the teachers who loathed them as symbols of unjust power, we could have worked together to achieve greater harmony on the island. After all, for at least eight hours a day, five days a week, we were locked up together.

The Voice

ENTRIES AND EXITS are always painful: They chafe and illuminate the diminished possibilities we're welcoming or leaving behind. My two lives clashed like dogs fighting dusk to dawn. Night was the secrecy of drag and smoke, she-males on stilettos tottering over cobblestones. Day was a ritual do-over, joining the crowds that swarmed the marble halls of Grand Central Terminal, the brass hands of its antique clocks slicing time into an illusion of steady flow. Against these barricades, aspirations diminished, their remainder paid forward, passed along to the next day. Then night returned, and time was again suspended.

I called Michelle from a payphone on the corner of 14th Street and heard distance in her crackling voice as though she were talking to me from a foreign country about my customer service problem. I washed my blue flower shirt and wore it again to Manitoba's, believing its talismanic power would draw Rocco and his entourage through the door. When they didn't appear, I'd descend the steps into Hellfire and chain myself into one of the stalls with Mistress Evil. Then without warning, Hellfire abruptly closed, a casualty in Mayor Giuliani's war to sanitize Manhattan. It would never be possible to completely scour the transgression from those concrete cellar walls, the desire written on flesh and carved into stone.

In the daylight hours, I could pretend to forget what I had lost. The voyeurs who lived in the apartments surrounding mine still watched me, masturbating as we exposed ourselves. A new tenant moved into the apartment directly across from mine, their window covered with venetian blinds that were sometimes raised several inches above the sill. One morning I was staring at their window, daydreaming about them watching me, needles of excitement prickling my chest and stomach. Suddenly, someone inside the apartment yelled, "What the fuck you lookin' at? I'll come over there and kick your ass."

I didn't believe what I'd heard and looked again at the window blinds beneath the fragile pane of glass. Never had anyone spoken to me from any of the facing apartments, as though it was understood that the dream of our gaze would be broken by a human voice. I listened, and again I heard a voice shout, "What you want?" a challenge obviously directed at me as though something inside of me had been projected onto the blank screen of the glass. Someone was seeing a part of me that I didn't want revealed, was peering beyond my skin and flesh, attempting to exorcize demons without my permission.

I felt rage. Deep, uncontrollable urges to kill that voice. Not just to kill it, but to punish it, torture it decibel by decibel into silence. What had been said, though, could not be unsaid. I had heard its message, and nothing could erase that. Never again would the fantasy of seeing and being seen be intact; a grain of anxiety had been introduced that would not disappear. It had been ruined by the voice. The voice that needed to be made an example of, pilloried, executed in the public square, documented and photographed as a warning to anyone who would follow it. I grasped why some guards would haul prisoners out of their cells at night and beat them bloody, then lock them in solitary confinement for ninety days. We were all prisoners, and those who broke the spell, the dream that kept us spinning in our tenuous orbits, needed to be destroyed. How else could we bear to look at our own reflection as we woke into a new day?

Reaching for the eight-inch hunting knife I'd bought from a silversmith booth in the Village when I'd first moved to the city, I stabbed it into the windowsill, its tip piercing the flaking paint and entering the soft wood. Shadows moved behind the blinds, and I knew that whoever was behind them was watching. I turned on my stereo and blasted death metal that shook the frame of the carriage house, praying that the person would appear. I wanted to see him, his ugly, angry face pulling the blinds apart as he stared back at me, squinting blue eyes and thin lips pulled back from yellowed teeth, acne scars pitting his cheeks. He wanted to see me, to shame me, but had he realized that the looking went both ways, the punishment he would receive so extreme that he would never want to speak again?

Over the next hour and a half, I returned to the window and grabbed the knife handle, staring at the neighbor's window. Turned the volume up on Lamb of God. Pulled out the knife, stabbed it again into the windowsill, chalky paint flaking onto my hand. I was entering some kind of trance, imagining I'd been convicted and released from Rikers, and if I didn't pull myself out, find a way to stop, I was going to walk across the courtyard, open the door of the neighboring building, climb the stairs to the second story, kick in the door, and stab this person to death in his new apartment. I wouldn't speak, not when he begged or asked why, not when he promised or apologized. The voice would be killed in silence.

The vividness of that thought woke me up. Not like an on/off switch. More like the gradual turning of a faucet. The neighbor did not raise his blinds. He did not shout again though I still felt his presence and knew he was a coward. A fucking coward who knew enough to protect his life. Finally, I lowered the volume on my stereo and removed the knife from the windowsill. My hands were shaking.

The chorus of the song echoed in my ears: *Destroy yourself, see who gives a fuck*. The ethos of death culture, of lone white shooters, homicidal incels, murder-suicides. The language of hate crimes against the self, against others. Self-hate weaponized. All connections with others, with history, blurred behind a wall of amnesia. This was not a language that I needed to learn: It had been given to me, had infected me, passed down through generations. I'd heard it when my father had pronounced the white officer not guilty, when the Hells Angels had surrounded me in the bar, in the blurry letters of the KKK fliers taped to telephone poles near my childhood home. When I recognized it, it was like looking into a mirror at a distorted image that demanded to be seen.

I was shocked that none of the other neighbors had called the cops to complain about the noise. Whoever it was who'd shouted at me from that apartment never showed his face, although I looked for him often, glancing at the window across from mine. Did he really exist? Had he moved, fled from what wanted to kill him? He had one advantage: He knew what I looked like though I'd never seen him. I could have passed him dozens of times in the street, even on the sidewalk outside the building, and I would not have recognized him. Not unless I heard him speak first, the sound of his voice as telling as a signature.

This faceless person, this disembodied voice, carried a message: My pain and what I did to conceal it from myself would kill me if I didn't look at it. Just as I understood the guard's desire to sustain the dream of incarceration, I grasped how men could become killers, how murderous rage was fed by hidden shame. When the person in the other apartment yelled at me, he exposed a secret about myself I couldn't bear to see and destroyed the illusion the secret rested upon. Once the secret was destroyed, I was flooded with all of the emotions it was designed to conceal. What had enraged me was not that he'd refused to play my game but that he'd exposed that darkness.

I was possessed by what I thought it meant to be a man, by the masculine codes I'd internalized not only mentally but also in my flesh, my father throwing me down the stairs, every beating I'd received, the ceaseless demand to be seen but not touched. When the defensive position I lived inside was exposed, I had learned to lash out, unable to see that this violence only increased my isolation, the illusion that I was separate from others, that if I was vulnerable they would attack me as mercilessly as I attacked myself.

I thought back to my original crime, the first time I could remember deliberately harming someone. I was five, my brother three years younger, and I scratched his face hard enough that it bled. Four long gouges from his forehead to his chin. My parents had told me never to do it again, and a couple weeks later I did the same thing, scratching his face again. After the second time, they told me that if I did it again I wouldn't be allowed to watch television for a month. That stopped me, but why had I scratched my brother in the first place? What had compelled me to do something so cruel and violent? And why had I repeated it, despite being punished? Why hadn't my parents asked me about my feelings, been curious about what was going on inside me? Instead, I learned another lesson about fear and self-control, one that had served me as well as it had the men I'd taught.

I'd stood in line for hours to get tickets for Shakespeare in the Park, that year featuring a production of *Mother Courage* starring Meryl Streep and Kevin Kline. The evening of the performance a deluge poured over the city, and Lauren suggested we stay home rather than brave the flooded paths to the stage in Central Park. I was adamant about at least attempting to see the play, so we dashed into a cab and ploughed uptown through inches of furious rain.

Once we reached the outskirts of the Park, we had to wade through the pitch-black labyrinth leading to the Delacorte Theater, detouring around surging water as our umbrellas buckled in the wind. Several times we considered turning back, but each step closer made the idea of quitting more impossible. The same feeling possessed me when I lay at night beside her, wanting to break up but terrified by the thought of our years together evaporating, all the struggle and hard-won truces erased.

Eventually we saw the glowing nimbus of stage lights and joined a group whose strangely elated faces reflected the same trial we'd experienced, all of us drenched animals lumbering up the ramp to Noah's Ark. Though the play was delayed for thirty minutes, we found ourselves in the third row, staring at Meryl Streep's muddy feet as she sat on a barrel of dynamite and serenaded the audience. I remember the end of her first song as Mother Courage sang,

> The new year's come. The watchmen shout.
> The thaw sets in. The dead remain.
> Wherever life has not died out
> It staggers to its feet again.

Although I often felt dead inside, something within me was struggling to live in the midst of the deadness, a struggle I also saw reflected every day on Rikers as the men entombed there fought the living death of their captivity. It was a heroic endeavor. Messy and conflicted, seemingly impossible. Unlike Mother Courage, I was not profiting from war or its related atrocities. I chose to work in prison, to traverse that border of suffering, but like her I was changed by it, eaten inside by what I had seen. Still, I vowed to keep returning.

Do-Over

SPRING ARRIVED, BRINGING buckets of crimson and violet poppies outside delis and flowering branches of trees arching above sidewalks. Fetid mounds of thawing prison garbage began to hiss and steam. I saw Jenna pushing a stroller across the street. She'd met someone, gotten pregnant, and moved to the island of Jamaica with him. They'd recently split and now she was back in her apartment with her new baby and, of course, Brujo. I remembered a conversation we had before she left me to return to her ex-con boyfriend. She said she wanted a baby and would go back with him if he wanted one, because it was obvious that I didn't want one. And I recalled her constantly pressuring me to sleep with her unprotected, which I agreed to do after nearly being stomped to death by Hells Angels. She'd gotten what she wanted, the baby and the pit bull together in her studio apartment, but without the father, the father I could have become.

Returning to GMDC, where I'd shadowed Paige three years earlier, felt strangely like a punishment. Stripped of my title as facility coordinator, I was clearly on Gloria's shit list. I understood; she was charged with the survival of Horizon and in that role she had to negotiate a very tenuous line between the needs of the school and the bureaucracy of the Department of Corrections. Teachers like me made this difficult. I'd left both the West Facility and GRVC after seriously challenging, and some may say undermining, the authority of the guards. I'd refused to play the political game, to conform to the whims of prison officials whose promises were best viewed as suggestions. I also had not communicated with her about my struggles and asked for her guidance, which would have shown my willingness to change.

Nights that I stayed at Lauren's apartment, I usually waited until she fell asleep and then slipped out from under the sheets, got dressed, and went roaming the bars on Second Avenue. The sidewalks were packed with people spilling out of Irish pubs that lined the street. Inside, a crush of bodies corralled around the bar lured me closer, women laughing and shouting to their friends, one of them turning to look up at me and smile. When I reached my arms around her waist she leaned into me, her eyes daring.

Several hours later I returned to Lauren's building, passing the bored doorman inured to my late-night sojourns, asleep on his chair as I entered the elevator, used my key to gently open the door, and attempted to crawl back into bed undetected, the smoky taste of the girl I'd kissed still in my mouth. Once, she woke up while I was pulling on my boots and said, No more, I won't let you stay here and keep leaving like this. After that I stopped, although my wandering continued on nights I spent in the carriage house, staggering bar to bar.

Early that summer Lauren asked me to move all of my things out of her apartment after she heard a voice message on my phone from a woman who asked me to help her film a documentary she was making about teaching in prison. I'm not sure why Lauren listened to that message, but probably the phone rang and I'd refused to answer it. It wasn't so much the content of the woman's message that gave away my intent, the *it was a pleasure to meet you last night* and *thank you so much for offering to help, call me soon,* as it was the tone in her voice, that mix of coyness and anticipation. I'd met her at the Red Room, and after listening to her desire to film a documentary on Rikers told her I could bring her inside, a ludicrous boast that Lauren could easily see through for what it was, a seduction.

Confronted with the truth, I played the last insidious card of liars, which is to feign ignorance of their intentions until the other person begins to doubt what they know is true. I swore I really did want to help this film student for purely altruistic reasons, that I felt an obligation to the prisoners to bring their story to the larger world, and so on. None of this worked. Although part of her may have wanted to believe my story, Lauren didn't buy it. I tossed the books and clothes that had migrated to her apartment into boxes and hauled them back to the carriage house.

My lies were caving in, and I had no escape from them. Living in the tiny room suspended three stories above ground, less than a mile away from the welfare hotel were I'd first landed on my own in the city, I was lost. It wasn't just that I was afraid that Rikers was infecting me with its captive rage or that my sexual fantasies would compel me to lose control, but that I would be alone with the punishing voice inside my head, helpless. There was relief in my lies' being exposed, in feeling that I was at the end of something, some cruelty that could not be sustained. What was true was that I no longer wanted to work at Horizon, no longer believed that I could give more than I would take. I was done.

Gloria didn't seem surprised when I walked into her office and sat across from her desk to tell her, I quit. She actually looked relieved. She did not argue as I knew she had with others who had attempted to resign, telling them that they needed to reconsider. Instead, she agreed that I would probably have an easier time teaching somewhere else. Her honesty was something I'd admired and trusted, and in difficult moments the most obvious statements of truth can sound comforting. I knew that she cared about me, and that she'd seen me struggling. It was a decision that all of my colleagues would eventually make: when to leave the island, when to surrender to the impossibility of continuing to swim against the stream.

Atlantis

THE EVENTS OF the next year, when this story ends, whirl and tremble in my mind's eye. Like the mirage of an Indian summer, fleeting warmth spread over me after I resigned, tension evaporating through the pores of my skin, through cracks in sidewalks and the blossoms of cherry trees. After several days a calm feeling enveloped me, the hum of my adrenal system powering down. Later came the nightmares, dreams of inmates pinning me against a wall and slashing my shirt into bloody streamers, night sweats, and waking afraid that someone had broken into the carriage house and was hiding in my bathroom. Unable to sleep, I'd dress and take a late-night walk through the Meatpacking District toward Hellfire, forgetting it was closed until I arrived at its shuttered doors.

I found another teaching gig at the Marta Valle School on the Lower East Side of Manhattan. The principal, Matt D'Agostino, was new and had been hired after a student had been stabbed to death the previous year in a school hallway. Following unwanted news media attention, the Board decided to fire all of the previous administration and to reassign many of the teachers, which usually meant sending them to some even less desirable outpost of educational dysfunction. Like the place I'd come from, for instance. Matt hired me after requesting that I demonstrate my teaching skills by delivering a ten-minute lesson. I talked about the ritual uses of tribal masks in Africa and metaphorical masks in the scene in *Macbeth* where he and Lady Macbeth discuss killing Duncan.

A few weeks later, he also made me a dean, which entailed giving me a radio and a bullhorn and charging me with maintaining order before and after school, during lunchtime, and whenever I had a free period during the day. The two other deans were also my height: one with long dreadlocks who looked exactly like Lennox Louis, the other with a mullet and rattail who was black Irish from the North Shore of Long Island. There were also two security guards stationed at a desk near the school entrance. When a fight erupted we'd all get a call over the radio that a "911" was occurring in a certain classroom or corridor, and we'd sprint to that location. My favorite part was the running, the rush of navigating the maze of hallways where the ghost of the dead teenager lingered. I'd watched riot guards on the island sprint in similar fashion toward whatever unknown violence awaited them. Every day after school we patrolled a three-block radius around the building looking for fights to disrupt.

My new students were tough kids, mostly Dominican and Puerto Rican, many of them in various gangs, but they weren't killers or sociopaths. Their parents could still come to teacher conferences and chew them out until they cried, and they still preferred my disciplinary measures to the wrath of their *abuelas* or *tias*. One girl told me her aunt had sent her mother a special paddle from the Dominican Republic to beat her with. I'm sure other teachers found the students impossibly difficult; the school averaged about two fights a day, every day. But to me they were much easier to deal with, much different from the classes I'd waged war with on Rikers. Here, no one called me a white devil, no one asked me to play the bathroom or threatened to beat me unconscious; instead, they often apologized when I called them outside the classroom.

The aftermath of leaving Rikers continued to resound, the clanging of sliding gates startling me from sleep or pulling me forward as I rode the subway, my thoughts a labyrinth of underground tunnels leading me back to the island. All cages are portable, constructed, and personal, nonexistent until someone inhabits them. I was still bound by invisible threads, one moment relieved I was no longer riding route buses to reach the island's deep interior and the next horrified by how this interior had followed and surrounded me, metastasizing to engulf the entire city.

I slept with the hunting knife beside my bed. Men still watched me through my windows. On my morning walks to Marta Valle from the West Village, I passed by a gigantic mural of a gloved fist smashing a bald man's jaw. Painted in thick black lines against a white backdrop, the perspective rendered the painting three-dimensional, as if the fist would continue to travel and strike the viewer. I remembered a phrase from Jean-Michel Basquiat's notebooks: *JIMMY BEST ON HIS BACK TO THE SUCKER-PUNCH OF HIS CHILDHOOD FILES.*

Matt asked me to talk to a student named Rafael who always spoke to me when I passed him in the hallways. Rafael was sixteen and still in ninth grade, and every day he wore a full leather outfit to school complete with a leather trench coat, leather pants, and leather motorcycle gloves. Eventually he began to stink so badly that students and finally teachers complained. Since Rafael was a big kid, energetic and quick to anger, they were afraid to confront him. Probably because I'd just left Rikers where inmates scared of being assaulted in the showers didn't bathe and where homeless men were brought in swathed in mummified layers of filth, I hadn't really noticed Rafael's stench. He wore his suit of armor and appeared oblivious to others' reactions, those rank leathers a second skin he moved inside freely.

One day as the last classes were dismissing I found Rafael and asked to talk to him. I gently asked him for a favor, saying that since his leathers were making some of the students uncomfortable maybe he could consider wearing something else to school. What I was saying to him silently was that I also needed a protective skin to face the world, and I did not want anyone to see what was underneath. Without words, he told me that he understood.

The next morning, he strolled through the school gates without his leather garb. Instead, he was dressed head to toe in desert camouflage, an outfit whose paramilitary edge made it a suitable substitute for his biker outlaw look. I smiled at him and we shook hands. Then I noticed, on one of his pants legs, a splash of what appeared to be white paint. I wondered whether he was secretly the artist who'd painted the enormous mural I walked by every day. I wanted to help kids like Rafael stay off the island, and to do that I needed to intervene before they could end up there, giving him a chance to rewrite his own childhood files so he believed that another life was possible.

We were more, however, than our files, childhood or otherwise. More than what we wrote or what was written about us, more than the visible parts of our lives or what we could understand about ourselves. Both on and off the island we survived, cycling in and out of a captivity that was sometimes imposed on us by ourselves, sometimes by others. Relentlessly compelled forward, all of us were doing the gift of time, fortunate to be alive despite the pain we endured. Searching for what had been lost, what was waiting to be found.

A few evenings later I was riding the A train uptown when I heard someone shout my name. I don't know why, but I instinctively stood up from my seat, turning toward the voice as a young man approached me.

"Mr. Lamson, it's Deonte. I don't know if you remember me, but you taught me on the island."

The young man smiled and reached out his hand. We shook. His dark, chiseled face was foreign to me, the face of a stranger, as though I couldn't recognize him outside of the place where we'd met.

"So, you're out now?" I asked lamely.

"Yes, I was released a few months ago. I just wanted to thank you. You helped me a lot in there."

I couldn't remember what I'd done to help. I wished I could.

"I'm glad. I'm happy to see you out in the city. Thank you so much for saying something to me."

I smiled at him and shook hands again before he turned and disappeared into the crowded car. I sat down again and felt like crying. I'd never seen one of my former Horizon students in the city, although I often hoped that I would, knowing that their cases were unresolved and that despite all of their disadvantages they could be found innocent. Seeing Deonte on the train confirmed that they all had other lives, and that despite my faulty memory, they remembered what we'd done together.

I was ashamed that I'd abandoned them because I had antagonized the guards and had allowed my fear and rage to control me. Above all, I was shamed by my secret life, by my trips to Hellfire and my dangerous exhibitionism that failed to remedy my self-loathing or assuage the need to be seen. My internal island was drowning, submerged beneath waves of compulsivity and shame, the cycle repeating until I was exhausted and couldn't breathe inside my own skin. I had to believe that a city still existed below those waters and that with guidance I could find it, a place of wholeness within myself fragile and imperiled yet intact.

When the shame momentarily subsided, I also thought about the inmates on Rikers, the ones I'd taught who were still there, confined on a floating island between Queens and the Bronx. Had I truly abandoned them, and if so, why? How would I explain it to them if we could meet again in a place outside prison walls? Could they forgive me, knowing that wherever I went, memories of them locked inside Rikers followed me, the vision of a lost Atlantis whose inhabitants shimmered in the distance, calling?

Finally, I resort to metaphor when describing the island as what it signifies overspills the words that try to contain it. In this sense, Rikers will never be closed. What it represents as a place of exile where all of society's dark dreams are banished is too powerful; if it did not exist, another such place would be constructed, an unreal city where human beings were imprisoned without recourse or appeal. Unseen and unheard, ciphers imbued with the meaning of all that we have done.

Epilogue

FIFTEEN YEARS AFTER leaving Rikers, I was lying on the floor of the prison chapel of the Ferguson Unit outside of Huntsville. A circle of inmates peered down at me huddled on the yoga mat as I demonstrated child's pose. I was half regretting the bravado of this gesture, having just met these men an hour ago, walked through the prison gates, beneath the brick guard tower, back inside. We breathed together in silence. I let gravity take me, let breath soften my tense shoulders and back. One of my Zen teachers said that we have backs like turtles when we first begin sitting, then gradually they soften, the protective shielding that covers our hearts becoming more porous.

Why was I there? Roshi Gaelyn Godwin, abbot of the Houston Zen Center, had asked me to accompany her to teach the prison *sangha* at Ferguson. The prisoners had sent letters to Buddhist organizations throughout Texas and she'd responded by offering to meet with them every Monday for a two-hour class. During these sessions they practiced sitting and walking meditation, then discussed Thich Nhat Hanh's book *The Heart of the Buddha's Teachings*. As we'd driven that morning past Huntsville, I had spotted a bloated hog dead in a ditch on the side of the road. I imagined it had escaped from one of the prisons and had been punished like one of the people in Greek myths transformed into animals. Desperate to escape, it had plunged across the road and been struck. Now I was following its path in reverse, walking through locked doors and sally ports, transitioning from beast to human once more, the walls of my internal cage touching the walls of these man-made cages. I was soothed and also terrified by the memories their contact evoked.

Texas was never on my radar. I'd never been there except to pass through the airport in Dallas. My writing had brought me there. Four years after leaving Rikers, I'd returned to my carriage house studio to see the light flashing on my answering machine. One new message. Pushing the button, I heard Tony Hoagland's voice congratulate me on being accepted to the creative writing program at the University of Houston. I'd applied to study with the phenomenal poets who were teaching there: Mark Doty, Claudia Rankine, Adam Zagajewski, and of course Tony. Stunned, I sat on the edge of my futon and played the message again. I was going to leave my job, give up my apartment, and move to Houston. I was going to follow Rilke's dictate to change my life more profoundly than I could have imagined.

Soon after arriving in Houston, I wandered into the Zen Center for morning meditation. A group of older folks dressed all in black sat on cushions facing the walls. I was shown where to sit. The bell rang. I followed my breath and stared at the play of light and shadow on the wall. After several minutes, waves of heat began rising from my belly to my chest. Sweat poured down my face as though a furnace door had been opened. My breathing felt shallow, constricted. I clung to the basic instruction: Sit and don't move. Return your attention to your posture and your breath. Every second was painful. I wanted to jump up, hurl my cushion, run from the room. When the bell rang again, I was drenched.

And lighter. Some pressure inside me had eased, revealing a glimmer of spaciousness. I didn't speak with anyone after sitting, never stayed for tea and socializing. I felt too tender afterward. Defenseless. I retreated, but I came back every weekend for another torturous round of sitting. The practice was flowing, finding whatever cracks and fissures it could enter and soften. Eventually, I spoke to someone and enjoyed it a little. I'd found a new doorway that led into a different way of being with myself and others. Weeks, months, years of practice continued to cultivate this way, leading to my current preparations to be ordained as a priest in the Soto Zen lineage by my teacher, Roshi Godwin.

In 2016, I served as the Summer Poet in Residence at the University of Mississippi. Driving from Houston to Oxford, I passed dozens of billboards advertising TRUMP. In nearby Memphis and in cities across the country, Black Lives Matter demonstrations were occurring. Finally arriving at the colonial mansion donated by John Grisham to the English Department, I settled into a routine—writing, teaching a few classes, and watching news about the protests. The violent, contested history of the beautiful land that surrounded me was palpable. I began writing this book, sifting through notes I'd written, searching for its narrative shape. Shortly before I returned to Houston, Alton Sterling was pinned to the ground and shot by police at a gas station in Baton Rouge. On my trip back I stopped in Baton Rouge and visited the makeshift altar erected at the gas station. That night I went to a local Zen temple and meditated and prayed. I felt a strong connection between this book and the movement for social justice and vowed to finish it.

Today, two-and-a-half years into the Covid pandemic, Rikers Island is still in operation. Every week I read new stories about the corruption, violence, and abuse that occurs there. Nevertheless, the mayor of New York City, a former police officer, recently reinstituted solitary confinement on the island. Despite his stated intention to follow the plan to close Rikers by 2027 and to replace it with borough jails, the mayor's tough-on-crime actions and proposed bail reform measures suggest otherwise. The city council members representing Manhattan and Queens have vocally protested the construction of city jails in their boroughs. Beneath the public posturing and rhetoric, Rikers remains.

What the politicians do not say is that Rikers serves a function both practically as a jail complex apart from the boroughs of New York City and psychically as a repository for all of our badness where we can exile people and forget about them and justify their inhumane treatment by appealing to our collective ideas about right and wrong. Rikers serves as a threat, a place that symbolizes everything we wish to separate ourselves from. It will not be easy to dismantle or to replace such a structure, a floating monolith that embodies the American criminal justice system itself.

Which brings me back to the prison chapel at Ferguson. Lying on a yoga mat on the floor, my chest pressed against my knees, I spoke to the men circled around me. "This is child's pose," I said, "a resting pose where you release all effort and breathe, letting your forehead touch the mat." I could not see them, but I knew that they were listening, possibly wondering what such unguardedness felt like, the sensation of vulnerability they had once experienced as children long ago.

Ever since I'd walked through the prison gates that day I had felt displaced, as though I'd entered a different atmosphere, my memories of Rikers dissipating as we walked down corridors to the prison chapel. The truth was, I recoiled from being there. I was angry at the guard who'd pointed the way but had not offered to accompany us. Waves of dust motes curled and writhed in the air over our heads, visible in the morning light that sifted through the bars. A line of inmates stared as we passed by. I was afraid, as though I'd gained a new sensitivity, a sense of precariousness I'd never had on the island where I'd been protected by my self-hatred. I did not want to be back inside and felt ashamed and surprised at my resistance. Wasn't I there to share my spiritual practice with these men whom I recognized, wishing I could have done so years ago on Rikers? A practice that had helped me to move more freely within my cages, and that I believed could do the same for them?

My good intentions did not soothe my body's response. The men were waiting for us, sitting in a circle partitioned by screens from groups of praying Christians and Muslims. Voices murmuring "Jesus Christ," "Allah," "deliver us." Gaelyn rang the travel bell she'd brought and we sat quietly, the tension in my shoulders and hands slowly diminishing. I opened my eyes and looked at each inmate as they gazed back at me.

ACKNOWLEDGMENTS

THE AUTHOR WISHES to thank Chris Brunt, Hayan Charara, Robert Cremins, Ed Pavlic, Henk Rossouw, Daniel Wallace, and Jessica Wilbanks.

Brandon Dean Lamson teaches creative writing and literature at the University of Texas at Austin. His first book, *Starship Tahiti*, won the Juniper Prize for Poetry and was published by the University of Massachusetts Press. He is also the author of a chapbook entitled *Houston Gothic* (LaMunde Press, 2007), and his recent poems have appeared in *Poetry Daily*, *Poetry Northwest*, and *Prairie Schooner*. Currently he is finishing a second book of poems that explores ecological crises in Western Appalachia. His articles about social justice and Buddhist practice have appeared in *Buddhadharma Quarterly*, *Tricycle* magazine, and *Speculative Non-Buddhism*.

EMPIRE STATE EDITIONS SELECT TITLES FROM EMPIRE STATE EDITIONS